What are People Sayir

"Kelly Falardeau is giving t release of 'Self-esteem Does reminds us how important self-love is for our own ... gives us the tools that we can use to build and strengthen our self-esteem through powerful testimonial. An inspirational page turner."

Troy Payne
International Best Selling Author
of 'The Road to Resiliency'

"When you meet Kelly for the first time, all you see is her radiant smile from across the room. Then as you get closer, you see her smile get wider and her beautiful green eyes shine a welcome at you. I've known Kelly for some time now and contributed to her first book.

Yes, frankly, I knew she had scars, but they never seemed to matter. The beauty that shines from within makes them pale and fade in the shadows. Kelly has an irrepressible sprit of joy and adventure and she makes you feel good when you are with her. In her case, for sure beauty does not come from a bottle, it comes from her heart.

This book should be on every little girl's reading list. For that matter, on her mother's too and then the two of them should talk about how to apply its wisdom in their lives."

Bob 'Idea Man' Hooey
www.ideaman.net

"When someone asks me the definition of resilience or esteem, my answer is a description of Kelly. Every page of this book offers the gift of hope, inspiration, and wisdom."

Charmaine Hammond,
International Speaker and
Best Selling Author On Toby's Terms.

"Kelly's book is an amazing canvass carefully prepared for building self-esteem. This book will not only make you laugh out loud as you learn but it will also inspire you to make changes in your life when you see yourself reflected in Kelly's words. Self-esteem is a choice, as Kelly teaches, and making the choice to live as a person of love rather than one of competition, or complaining, is powerful. Every human being needs to hear that

self-esteem doesn't come in a bottle. Kelly's candid view of taking responsibility for your own inner joy comes out of her personal experiences. Her words give you the feeling she understands where you might be on your journey and how to get through it in style. If you allow her words, her sense of humor and her love to reach into your heart as you read, then you will come away from this book with a huge take-a-way that can bring you to the next level of personal joy. Only YOU can decide if you will practice Kelly's advice, but no matter what, her entertaining and educational look at self-esteem is a MUST read - not only once - but twice!"

Kellie Frazier
www.ConnectingFHL.com

"Each moment you have the opportunity to be more of the real you. Make a solid commitment to deepen your relationship with yourself and align with your truest nature. Instead of defining yourself with a list of yesterday's standards, begin to reflect toward the empowered features of the woman you are now. In Kelly's book, you'll find the answers to bring the most amazing you to life!"

Marsh Engle
www.MarshEngle.com

"I just finished reading Kelly's book and all I can say is "Wow!" I don't know how she does it, but she always finds a way to really cut down to what really matters. How can you not take self-esteem advice from a woman who, despite a body covered in scars, gets out there front-and-center and takes on the world? After reading this book, I feel as if all of Kelly's self-confidence has somehow given a boost to my own. Her step-by-step instructions in each chapter really made me think about how I'd been treating myself and some of the negative thoughts I've let seep slowly into my psyche. I look at myself differently now. I AM beautiful -- gorgeous in fact. And I have Kelly to thank for that."

Tara Geissinger
www.onlineprnews.com

"Kelly's chapters will inspire you to laugh, reflect and give yourself a break. Her writing style is conversational, so you can flow through the pages just as comfortably as if you were sitting on the couch in her living room having coffee with her. Self-Esteem Doesn't Come in a Bottle is a sincere, authentic and beautiful compilation of self-esteem wisdom, just like Kelly."

Lisa Litwinski
www.litpathlearning.com

"What an awesome read! Your book offers numerous insights into esteem / self-esteem augmented so extremely well by 'your story' ... your life experiences! It offers many practical and hands-on techniques into which the reader can sink his/her teeth. You've written your book both in a language and format that would appeal to the wide majority of the population and certainly to anyone struggling with esteem issues. HUGS to you for a job very well done!"

Murray Douglas

Self-Esteem
Doesn't
Come in a Bottle

Kelly Falardeau

Copyright 2011 by Kelly Falardeau
Published by Falardeau Productions

ISBN: 978-1466295834

1st Edition

All rights reserved, including the right to reproduce this work in any form whatsoever, including digital, without permission in writing from the publisher, except for brief passages in connection with a review.

Disclaimer: This is a true story, and the characters and events are real. However, in some cases, the names, descriptions, and locations have been changed, and some events have been altered, combined or condensed for storytelling purposes, but the overall chronology is an accurate depiction of the author's experience. You may also be uncomfortable with some of the language and content.

Cover design by Dianna Bowes www.fabulousat50.com
Cover photography by Nicole Ashley www.nicoleashley.ca
Edited by Murray Douglas/Ashley Raffard
Illustrations by Katherine Augade
Kelly is available to speak at events and to contact her:
Website: www.mykellyf.com or blog: http://blog.mykellyf.com

k@

Dedication

This book is dedicated to my awesome kids,
Alexanna, Cody and Parker:

*"The secret to great self-esteem
is to learn how to make
yourself feel great,
not like crap."*

~Kelly Falardeau

k@

Note from the Author

Why the title, "Self-Esteem Doesn't Come in a Bottle?" This title really hit home for me for a few reasons. I was in a writing workshop and one of the tasks we were assigned, was to help each other come up with titles and taglines for our new books. Originally, I had picked something else for a title. I wasn't in love with it, but thought it was good enough.

When it was time to create the taglines, Janice Graham said to me, "How about self-esteem doesn't come in a bottle" as a tagline? And I said, "Aha, that's it, I love it!"

I absolutely loved my tagline that she came up with. The next day with much thought, if I love the tagline so much, why don't I make it the title, and so that's what I did.

The reason this title suits me is because it reminds me of all the times people have come up to me telling me that they have a miracle for my scars. They have something that will take my scars away or they have something that will make me beautiful. What they don't realize is that I don't need my scars to disappear or be covered up. **I've learned how to fall in love with me - scars and all.**

I haven't worn make-up since I was 20-years-old. For some reason, make-up doesn't make me feel beautiful; it doesn't give me the "wow" factor that it gives some women. The stuff in the bottle wasn't the answer for me to have great self-esteem; it's the laughing, the sense of accomplishment, the loving the little parts of me; the compliments, my passion, wearing heels with my hot ass jeans. It's about wearing pigtails even with a bald spot showing, it's about seeing my big gorgeous green eyes when I look in the mirror. It's all those little things that make me feel greater than great. It was all that,

that taught me how to feel great about me, not the magic stuff in the bottle that never worked.

Another thing that makes me feel great is when I hear compliments about my kids and how well behaved they are. Or when I hear my one twin say to the other twin, *"Wow, are you ever great at that!"* I love hearing my kids empowering each other.

Another time I felt great was when my daughter Alexanna said to me, *"Mom, you and Katy Perry are the biggest inspirations in my life."* That brought me to tears knowing that I inspire my daughter. It gave me one more thing to feel great about. She gave that gift to me right when I was feeling tremendous guilt about making a life change and ending my marriage of 24-years. *Thank you Alex; you gave me that gift right when I needed it the most.*

Do you honestly think that little bottle will make me or you feel beautiful? I don't think so. I know where my self-esteem comes from and there aren't enough bottles in the world to make that happen.

So how do I do it? Everyone wants to know the 'how.' I remember talking to Linda Franklin of the Real Cougar Woman and she lives in New York, a city where self-image is very important. We talked for an hour and she said, *"Kelly, seriously, how do you walk out the door with scars all over your body? I want to know your secrets."* And that got me thinking, do I have secrets to my self-esteem? And if so, what are they?

And so, that's what this book is all about, it's my secrets to the 'how.' And the great thing is my ultimate secret was already revealed on the dedication page. If you can learn how to do that, I promise you, you will feel greater than great. My secrets are real-world things I've done and I know they will work for you too if you apply them.

The best part is, they're just "little" things, but if you can master even three or four of my secrets on a consistent basis, you will notice a *certain* change.

My other advice to you is that when you have a dream, you have to go for it, no matter how big or small. You can't let obstacles stop you from achieving what you want in your life. You have to find a way to overcome them. The obstacles are just there to see how you handle them and to what extent you're willing to go to get what you want. A lot of times, an obstacle is put in front of you to steer you in another direction, and usually a more 'correct' one. Obstacles are also meant to be an opportunity not a stumbling block.

A publisher told me they didn't think I had enough of a story to write my first book 'No Risk No Rewards'. Do you think I let that little 'no' stop me? Absolutely not! I knew there were people who wanted to hear my story and would buy my book, I wasn't going to let anyone stop me from writing my first book, no way, no how!

I found a way to make it happen. I self-published it and only bought as many books as I could afford. I got my friends involved who helped me with the content, editing and the cover. I sold it on the internet and at speaking events and I'm happy her 'no' didn't stop me dead in my tracks.

In fact, her 'no' encouraged me to do it even more. I wanted to prove to myself that I could write a book and that I did have enough content. Don't let one 'no' stop you from achieving your dreams. Can you imagine if Babe Ruth would have stopped playing baseball on his first strikeout? He kept trying until he got home runs and then he hit the record for the most home runs. I bet he's glad he didn't quit. Quitting sometimes isn't an option.

I wasn't given an option to quit. I've been turned down to dance by at least a thousand guys. Do you think I would have found my husband if I would have stopped asking guys to dance? In fact, he turned me down a couple times too. He just didn't feel like dancing to the song I wanted to dance to. It wasn't me personally; he just happened to hate the songs I liked.

Also included in my book are action steps you can take to start digging into your life and help you realize what you can do to make change. There is also a companion Action Guide you can purchase to go with this book so you can keep all your action steps together.

I want to thank Max, the ultimate man in my life, who supported me for the past 24-years and encouraged me to love, grow and discover the true me. *Max, thank you for that and thank you for giving me the wonderful kids that we have. I wouldn't have become the woman I am today if I didn't have you in my life. I know I can be challenging to deal with, but I'm doing what I know how to do best and that's to be stubborn, crazy, and a dreamer.*

I also want to thank the many friends and family who have helped me with my book and helped me to bring it to life, you know who you are and I'm afraid to list them here because I don't want to forget anybody. You are all very important to me and without you; I wouldn't have discovered this book and my secrets. *Thank you for encouraging me and supporting me to make this book come to life and thank you for contributing in every way possible.*

I hope you enjoy reading my book as much as I enjoyed writing it. Each chapter is based on a 'how', a how to develop great self-esteem. A few days ago, I read something on Facebook and it said, **you will only be successful if you share your knowledge with others and so that is what I'm doing, sharing my self-esteem secrets.**

((Hugs))

Kelly

Table of Contents

Foreword by Darren Jacklin   13

Introduction   15

How do you Develop Great Self-Esteem?   18

Quit Calling Yourself Names   20

Learn to Love Your Little Parts   25

Give out Selfless Gifts   29

Don't Postpone Joy   35

Associate with Empowering People   46

Learn How to Laugh at Yourself   54

Smile and Smile Some More   62

Realize Even the Weeds are Beautiful   68

Follow the Law of Reciprocation   73

Don't Sweat the Little Things   79

Purpose + Passion = Power   86

Find your Inspiration   90

Set Yourself up for Success, Not Failure   100

Find Your Gifts You Can Share   106

Celebrate Your Little Successes   114

De-clutter Your Head   119

Walk with your Head Held High   124

BONUS Chapter from Marsh Engle   133

BONUS Chapter from Jack Zufelt   136

Here's What I Know   140

FOREWORD

This book is about building your self-esteem and what it really takes to build it. It's time someone tells you straight, without any fluff and Kelly is the person to do it. A burn survivor who struggled with her beauty and self-esteem throughout her whole life, she's the perfect person to tell you that self-esteem doesn't come in any kind of bottle.

You've been bamboozled for too long and it isn't working for you. There is no magic pill, secret code, or quick fix when it comes to building up your self-esteem. You won't make $350,000 this year watching some late night television infomercial telling you that you can work for only four hours in a week and make you feel totally rich, full and delicious. You can't expect to build your self-esteem that way.

You are not going to look at yourself in the mirror one day and desire to have self-esteem. As you stand there, the phone rings and it's your best friend who just joined some business. She calls to invite you to join this business opportunity meeting where you can set up your own home based business and sell products out of your car's trunk. People can buy your product and rub some magic cream on their body to lose weight. You don't get rich and you won't build your self-esteem as fast as they lose 40 pounds in a week.

It would be great if you could go down to your local health food store and buy your 'self-esteem' in a beautifully wrapped bottle. You can't even buy some magical bubble bath with candles, chocolate and wine and build your self-esteem that way.

We are constantly bombarded with false advertising that makes us feel less, not good enough, and depressed. They make us feel that we have some kind of anxiety disorder, or we are not beautiful enough; just so the advertisers can guilt us into buying their product or services.

We've lost sight of the simple but profound fundamentals of what it takes to build up your self-esteem.

You will learn in this book that your attitude determines your altitude. You will learn that it's not what happens to you in your life but it's what you choose to do about it.

Let the words in this book touch you, move you and inspire you into action into building up your own self-esteem. If you are a woman, you can let your radiance, light and energy shine brightly and if you are a man, you can live from your deep truth, purpose and passion.

I look forward to our paths crossing and meeting one day in person.

With deep love and respect from your friend,

Darren Jacklin
World Class Professional Speaker,
Corporate Trainer, Author
www.DarrenJacklin.com

INTRODUCTION

Who said self-esteem comes in a bottle? What makes us think that putting on make-up or using an anti-aging cream or having chemicals injected into our faces is going to give us great self-esteem? Seriously, what is it that makes us think that feeling great comes in a bottle?

And since when did self-esteem come in a bottle of beer or alcohol? You might get some temporary 'liquid courage', but it will never build your self-esteem into a long lasting relationship.

I learned a long time ago that there was no magic cream or any magic surgery that was going to erase my scars and make them disappear. As much as I wanted to wake up scarless and beautiful, it wasn't going to happen no matter how much I prayed to God every night.

Many nights, when I would go to bed, I would pray and say, *"Dear God, please don't make me wake up in the morning and if I do have to, could I at least wake up without scars on my face so that I can be pretty like all the other girls please? Thank you."*

I had a choice, I could wallow in pity and feel sorry for myself and my ugly scarred-up body, or I could find another way to feel great about myself and not let my scars get in the way. I deserved a life just like any other scarless pretty girl. I deserved to feel great no matter what I looked like. I didn't need some 'beautiful' person telling me that I wasn't beautiful enough to have a life. I didn't need to hear from one more person saying to me that they would **never** go out in public looking like me.

I learned to accept my crooked arm, crooked fingers, deformed little ear, missing nipple, scarred face, big lips, bald spotted head, scarred arms, chest and back. Overall, I learned to accept my imperfect body as near-perfect enough for me. I learned to love myself for who I really am. And, that is me... That in itself, I discovered is beautiful and unique.

I deserved to have every opportunity in life just like any other kid. And my family didn't hold me back from anything. Not once did my family say I couldn't do something because I had scars on my body. Not once did my siblings get to do something that I didn't just because I was different from them, or because they deserved it more than me. I wasn't given an option to quit just because I had scars. It was like my whole family completely forgot I was burned. It just didn't matter to them. I was still beautiful, scars or no scars.

This book is all about how I developed a strong and healthy attitude and how there was no magic bottle that was going to give me the self-esteem I needed in order to walk out the door no matter what I looked like. I learned to find my self-esteem in my heart and soul, not in a bottle and I hope this book will do the same for you too. This book is full of my secrets that I developed over my years of growing up and discovering myself.

Now I should explain, the beginning, how I got burnt. When I was two-years-old, we lived on an acreage and my cousins were burning shingles from the old barn roof. A spark from the fire came out and landed on my clothes and I was engulfed in flames. I suffered third degree burns to 75% of my body. I wasn't expected to live and even had a near-death experience in the hospital. I spent three-months in the hospital and had surgeries every two years right up until I was 20-years-old. My first book 'No Risk No Rewards' has more details about my traumatic accident and how I went from near-death to success.

I wanted to write this book because every week I get emails from people asking me how I'm able to feel great about myself even with the scars. Women email me all the time saying they feel crappy and not sure how to feel good about themselves. They don't understand how I can do it and they can't.

I get mothers who say to me, I wish I would have brought my daughter to hear you speak; she needed to hear from you. She is so concerned about her body and relies on her friends' opinions and doesn't think she is beautiful or worth it.

It really bothers me when I get those emails because I believe that everyone has an inner beauty and that counts more than outer beauty. I am really passionate about helping others to feel great and to not be so hard on themselves, and concerned with what others think of them.

HOW DO YOU DEVELOP GREAT SELF-ESTEEM AND FEEL GREATER THAN GREAT?

One thing I know for sure is that my self-esteem didn't develop overnight. It took many years of learning and discovering 'me' and who I am and what I do differently than others. It took many hours to discover what my "secrets" were. It also took me courage to realize that I didn't have to live the way other people did and that I could say 'no' and I could also say that I didn't believe what other people say as the truth. It was ok to not do things the way everyone else did and be different.

I discovered the way to develop great self-esteem is to do the following 17 things:

- Quit calling yourself names
- Learn to love your little parts
- Give out selfless gifts
- Don't postpone joy
- Associate with empowering people, develop Champions and Mentors
- Learn how to laugh at yourself
- Smile and smile some more
- Realize even the weeds are beautiful
- Follow the Law of Reciprocation
- Don't sweat the little things
- Purpose + Passion = Power
- Find your inspiration
- Set yourself up for success, not failure
- Find your 'gifts' you can share
- Celebrate your little successes

- De-clutter your head
- Walk with your head held high

Each chapter explains how you can do each step, along with action steps and a secret from me and a secret or two from a friend of mine.

There is also a companion Action Guide that you can purchase to keep all your action steps and secrets together.

Dear Kelly,

My self-esteem secret takes a little of that, a dash of this, then mix and blend well together. There really is no recipe for healthy self-esteem except the one you make over and over that works and fits best for you. A few ingredients I believe are an absolute necessity to great self-esteem are:

1) Honesty is like flour. You can't make most bread without it, and your self-esteem will never get better if it's missing. Never EVER lie to yourself as if you do you will never have a good starting point to get better. You will only wobble back and forth and fail. A stronger base will equal stronger longer lasting results.

2) Interview and consistently ask yourself questions, more importantly ANSWER your questions. For example, 'How do I feel about my self-worth today? No matter the answer feel good about being honest and being self-aware. Millions of people never EVER take the steps to be so strong.

3) Choose an action that will push you to feel any form of accomplishment. For example, 'The next time I look in the mirror I will notice something great about myself', 'My goal today is to notice three good physical and three great character things about just being me.'

Carefully mix and blend well together for 15-minutes each day, turn on high after watching it rise!

Amanda Welliver
www.paradigmesteem.com
Host of 'Paradigm Shift Radio' – A Self-Esteem Journey.
2010 Stevie Woman Entrepreneur of the Year for Canada
2006 YWCA Woman of Distinction Winner

CHAPTER 1

QUIT CALLING YOURSELF NAMES

It's time for you to stop calling yourself names - you know, those mean and negative names you use to describe yourself. You know what I mean - the names you call yourself that hurt you, like I'm so fat or I'm so ugly, or I'm so stupid, or I'm an idiot, or I've got such a big nose, or I'm such a loser. These names do absolutely nothing to help you; in fact, they hurt you, tremendously.

Do you remember how horrible you felt when someone called you a mean name when you were in school? So why do you do it to yourself? Why do you call yourself ugly, or stupid or retarded or whatever else you say to hurt yourself?

Every time you call yourself a name, it is reinforcement to your brain that yes, you are that, and your brain believes it because you keep saying it, so it must be true.

STOP IT! RIGHT NOW! Stop calling yourself names. You hate it when kids call each other names and you make them stop, so why don't you stop too? Your negative name calling is only hurting you more and more every day. No wonder you can't feel great about yourself. You keep telling yourself how crappy you are!

Start learning to call yourself great names - I promise you, you will feel better about yourself when you learn to call yourself happy positive names and not negative ones.

For example, when I was a teenager and called myself the ugly scar-faced girl, all I saw was how ugly my scars were. All I could see when I looked in the mirror was all my scars. They seemed to pop out more and that was all I noticed about myself. I kept noticing how ugly they were and therefore I was ugly too because I had the ugly scars on my face, arms and body.

I hated seeing pictures of myself because my scars made me look so ugly and I stopped letting people take pictures of me because as far as I was concerned I was ugly and there was no way you could convince me otherwise because I really believed that I was ugly.

When I started noticing and paying attention to my big green eyes and my cute nose, all of a sudden, when I looked in the mirror, those features popped out at me more and I started saying to myself, "*Wow, I have great eyes and a cute nose.*"

My scars started fading into the background and the features I loved about me started popping out. In fact, one day I even looked down at my arms and said "*Wow, where did those come from? I really do have scars on me; I forgot about that, I got burnt.*"

And seriously, that's the truth, I actually forgot I had scars on me; I forgot I was burnt.

When I was school-aged, I still remember going to my Nana's house (we had two houses on the acreage and I was very fortunate to be able to live across the driveway from my grandparents, the same acreage that I got burnt on) and every day she would put lamb oil on my bald spot (she was determined to make my hair grow back, but it never did) and then she would say "*Kel, those little scars on your cheeks remind me of little leaves. You have cute little leaves on your cheeks.*" I'll never forget that, she was trying to help me love my scars, not hate them.

One night, I was at a going away party for my friend Paul and his wife Cindy. Paul and I were talking and I was saying how different it was to be single (Max, my husband and I had separated a few months earlier) and feeling a little insecure about it. He said to me, "*Kel, you just have to look in the mirror and look at those eyes and say WOW, those eyes! You have WOW eyes and I'm not kidding.*"

My best friend told me three-years ago that he still remembered my hot ass from high school. I was shocked - I didn't know he thought that, but what a great compliment. See, I do have some great features, I'm not ugly.

I used to call myself the ugly scar-faced girl; now I call myself the gorgeous girl with the hot ass. And whenever I send a girlfriend a birthday wish on Facebook, I always say, "*Have a great birthday Gorgeous.*" Who doesn't like to be called gorgeous? I love it. When you call yourself great names, you learn to feel it.

ACTION STEPS:

Pay attention to the names you're calling yourself and write them down. Write down the good names and the bad ones.

Find a way to turn those negative names into positive names.

SECRET:

Find great names to call yourself and wipe those negative names out of your head.

Hi Kel,

Self-esteem, huh? Good grief, why couldn't you start with something a bit easier like world peace?!

We all experience self-doubt at some point in our lives – we're not pretty enough, smart enough, affluent enough, as important, as connected...blah, blah, blah. At the end of the day, I believe those are just excuses we make to ourselves as to why we can't or haven't achieved something. I think it goes back to that whole Yoda thing, "Do or do not. There is no try."

To me, self-esteem really comes down to what motivates you. Big secret here, but my prime motivator is fear (how you get me to admit these things publicly is beyond me-sheesh!).

Not the fear of actually doing something, but the fear of NOT doing it. I am far more afraid of regrets, or of looking back and wondering, "What if?" I simply want to know the answer – good, bad or otherwise. If the answer is "yes," yahoo, you're on your way. If the answer is "no," then rip it like a band-aid, learn from it and move on. People give far too much power to that two-letter word than is warranted. I'm not saying go in unprepared. Take some calculated risks and do your homework. And remember you're just like everyone else; you put your pants on one leg at a time too.

Something else I learned on the road to preserving self-esteem is that speed is the key to getting past rejection. Not everyone is going to like you, not everyone is going to want to buy your product. Move on to others who do, or find something else. Quickly. The faster you do this, the more successful you will be.

BTW, I read an interesting story about Lady Gaga who says, "When I wake up in the morning, I feel like any other 24-year-old insecure girl, then I say, 'Bitch, you're Lady Gaga, you get up and walk the walk today.'"

So, if even Lady Gaga struggles with self-esteem, then we can all put on our big-girl panties and woman up...

Be fabulous,
Janeen Norman
www.fabulouscorp.com

Dear Kelly,

My secret to great self-esteem is pushing myself physically...in all sorts of different ways. Healthy sports was my strength growing up; and the ability to use my body and my physical strength still gives me great confidence and shows me what I am capable of.

Lisa Chell
www.ultimateclarity.com

ॐ ॐ ॐ

Dear Kelly,

If I was to tell you I had the secret to self-esteem, I would be on Oprah right now and being sought after by every self-help organization to share the secret. I do not know the secret, but I know the first step to start heading in.

The true test is to ask yourself, are you the same person when in front of people as you are in private? This takes a deep honesty for some people. I believe self-esteem is simply knowing who you are for real. When you know something without any doubt, you hold all the power.

For example, if you told me that my son was not my son I would simply laugh and disagree. But if I had any level of doubt that he was not my son, I probably would be defensive or try to prove my position. This is the difference of "knowing something" and "believing something." If you believe you have self-esteem but you find yourself defending your position or trying to prove you are right; I would question the fact that you understand your true value. If you know who you are, you simply do not do these things.

The more you see who you are and stop manufacturing the person you want everyone to think you are, and just be you, with all the good and all the bad; this is the first step to self-esteem and even more inner peace.

Ben Oosterveld
www.youtube.com/user/BenOosterveld
www.twentynewclients.com

CHAPTER 2

LEARN TO LOVE YOUR LITTLE PARTS

"Give yourself permission to feel beautiful, look in the mirror and tell yourself you are HOT! Because you are!"
~ Kelly Falardeau

When you focus on what you love about yourself, you learn to love who you are. When you focus on what you hate about yourself, you learn to hate yourself.

For example, as I was growing up, I always hated my big lips. My doctor told me that if I sucked on my bottom lip, it could possibly make my lip smaller and so I did that all day every day, but that never worked.

Why should I let one thing I hate about myself affect my whole being? Just because I have a big lip, that doesn't mean I should hate my whole body. Just because I have a little deformed ear, that doesn't mean I should hate my whole body either. Those are just two small parts of me - I have other parts that are lovable and beautiful.

My mom told me how my doctor tried to fix my ear and make it look like my other one, but it didn't work. Apparently what happened is that when I first got burnt and they were debriding the burnt skin off my body, the resident doctor ended up cutting off the tip of my ear accidentally. Twice, my doctor tried removing skin from my legs to form a new ear, but both times it contracted down leaving me with my little deformed ear.

When I was younger, yes, I admit, I didn't like it much. It affected my hearing plus it was difficult to have pierced earrings with that ear and I was ashamed of my ugly deformed ear. I always tried to hide my little ear by wearing my hair down. I never wore pony tails as a kid because I didn't want others to see my ugly deformed ear. Some times when I wear headphones, they don't sit properly, and sunglasses usually look crooked on me, but oh well, it could be way worse.

At one time, I decided that I should check into getting a new prosthetic ear made so that it would look like my other ear. I thought the new ear would make me look more beautiful. But then I thought what if I don't like my new ear? Will I be able to have my little ear back? And no, I wouldn't be able to and I decided I couldn't live without my little ear. That ear was a part of me, something I had lived with all my life. How could I change my little ear, just to look beautiful for someone else and just so that other people looking at me would see that I looked normal?

I love my big green eyes. Some times when I look in the mirror, I just say to myself, "*Wow, you do have great eyes.*" I've given myself permission to feel great about myself. I don't have to blast it to the world and make it seem like I'm bragging, I just keep saying it to myself. I deserve to feel great and I deserve to tell myself. I don't need to wait for someone else to tell me I have great eyes. Why can't I tell myself I have great eyes when I believe I do? I can and so I do. I tell myself and as a result, **I build my own self-esteem and build my own belief system about myself.**

There are also times when I put on my jeans that I love and I look in the mirror and say to myself, "*Wow, you're looking great in those hot ass jeans today.*" Why shouldn't I compliment myself? Again, it's all about permission; **give yourself permission to tell yourself that you feel great**.

My advice is to find ways to love yourself and not just physical outer things about your body, but things you do and inner qualities. For example, I learned to love my laugh. So many people have said that they love when I laugh. It brings joy to them when they hear me laugh.

When I was at my friend Lee Horbachewski's 40th birthday party, we were having dinner with a few girlfriends and Lynne MacQuarrie said to us, "*Kel, I just love your laugh, if I ever become a stand-up comedian, I want you in my audience because I love your laugh and it's contagious and everyone around you will want to laugh too.*" Of course, I laughed even more because Lynne did a great imitation of Elaine from the Seinfeld show. She has the hair, the look and can even do the "Elaine Dance." I noticed too, no matter what, that I can laugh at the little things as well as the big things.

I also love when I'm passionate about something. When I have passion, I'm unstoppable and I don't quit until I'm done. When I have passion, I also can't sleep and my mind goes a million miles an hour. I also know that when I have passion, I get things done and accomplish things. The more I accomplish, the greater my self-esteem becomes. You don't need to love everything about yourself in order to love YOU. You just have to let the parts you do love shine more in your life.

ACTION STEPS:

Write down five things you love about yourself and if there's more, then write those down too, but find at least five. Give yourself permission to feel great about you. Do whatever gives you the "wow" factor. Put on your best outfit that makes you feel fantastic, do up your hair and make-up if that also makes you feel fantastic and look in the mirror and say "*Wow, I look great today.*"

SECRET:

Give yourself permission to love your little parts and tell yourself you feel great.

Dear Kelly,

My secret to great self-esteem is partly achieved by finding peace within, acceptance of my character defects, being comfortable and loving myself in my own skin.

Lily Chatterjee
Fellow Burn Survivor

ॐ ॐ ॐ

Dear Kelly,

If these were the last words I could ever say or write about self-esteem, I'd say… "Dig deep inside your soul, because self-esteem comes from deep inside, knowing that you are loved, you are created to be an amazing individual and that you have everything you need to make it through the tough stuff of life." You have the intelligence, the fortitude, the problem-solving ability, strength and the emotional stability to move forward despite the mountains, potholes, challenges or difficulties you might face.

To discover our intrinsic ability to garner that strength and fortitude to overcome whatever lies ahead, we need to recall and even sometimes relive those things we thought we couldn't possibly endure, much less succeed or rise above. In looking at the past, we gain confidence to face the future.

Self-esteem is not a magic potion, formula or strategy to propel us forward into the river of life. Self-esteem is realizing that we needn't cower in anger, fear, regret or timidity as we face the challenges in our path. Self-esteem is that joy deep inside that says "I can stand tall in who I am as I face what lies ahead. I may not do everything perfectly, but I will face each challenge with all my strength and ability and with a positive attitude that says, "I can make it through this."

Annette Stanwick©2011
Author, Inspirational Speaker and Freedom Facilitator
www.annettestanwick.com

CHAPTER 3

GIVE OUT SELFLESS GIFTS

"It makes me feel great knowing that I find the good in people, not the bad." ~ Kelly Falardeau

The single most selfless **gift** you can give someone is a compliment. I call it a gift because it's something you give to someone with no expectations and you can't take it back. When you give this gift to someone, it makes you feel great.

Think about it - how does a compliment make you feel? How great does one little compliment feel? How horrible does one negative comment feel? Compare the two and determine which is going to make you feel better about yourself? Which comment is going to build you up and which is going to bring you down?

One day at Walmart, the checkout girl said to me *"Do you ever have pretty eyes!"* I said, *"Thank you."* Do you know what happened? Two things. Her comment to me made me feel great plus made me smile all day. All day I was thinking how nice it was that she complimented me. I realized that compliments are the simple most selfless '**gifts**' you can give someone.

Another time I was watching a video of myself speaking. I was a little confused by it and thinking, wow, is that really what I look like, I look different than what I thought I looked like? So I texted my best friend and told him what I was doing and said, *"Is that really what I look like?"* and he said, *"Yes, beutiful you."* (Yes, I know it's spelled incorrectly, but he has horrible spelling and I knew what he meant, so it didn't matter).

I had this giant smile on my face and thanked him for the compliment.

And just like the Walmart girl, his little selfless gift made us both happy and feeling great about ourselves.

There is something else he also taught me and that is you're always supposed to accept and receive a compliment because if you don't, you make the person feel bad for complimenting you and eventually they stop doing it.

I can't remember what I said after his compliment, but I do remember him saying; *'you shouldn't say that because you make the person who gave you the compliment feel bad'*.

So whenever it's your turn to receive a compliment, say thank you. That's it. Don't downplay the compliment and make it seem like you don't deserve it because you do - otherwise the person wouldn't have complimented you. **Receive it and own it and love it that someone noticed something great about you. Enjoy it and allow yourself to feel great with this selfless gift!**

Now, as much as I love receiving compliments, I also love giving compliments. I don't hesitate to tell someone (even if I don't know them), that their hair looks great or that I love their outfit or whatever I feel. I learned that in order to receive compliments, I also needed to give them.

For example, my friend Shannon Berry and I were having dinner in a restaurant. Our server was this gorgeous young lady who I could tell was feeling a bit insecure about her job and abilities. I noticed that she had great inquisitive eyes and a beautiful smile and so I told her that I loved her smile.

You could tell she didn't get many compliments and she thanked me and all of a sudden she had a new confidence about herself. She was also able to do her job more confidently because she knew we were happy, easy going ladies who wanted to be her friend not judge her abilities. She also knew that we were treating her as an equal and not as someone different because she was a waitress. She was a gorgeous young lady who deserved the compliment.

A lot of times when people look at us, we seem to think they're thinking negatively about us, but that isn't always true. People are very quick to perceive something that may or may not be true.

Compliments are those little gifts we often forget about that make us feel great about ourselves. I also love compliments because they help me to figure out if an outfit or hairstyle really does look good on me. I seriously don't have that gift of knowing if an outfit really does suit me. I rely on other people's compliments to help me.

My cousin was also telling me about a time he was in Walmart and he told a girl, "*Hey when was the last time someone in Walmart told you how hot you are? Have a great day*" and he walked out. He wasn't flirting with her, he was complimenting her and he felt great giving her that gift. People don't get enough compliments in life. We're very quick to judge and criticize someone, but we're very slow in complimenting and empowering others to feel great. **The more we empower others, the more empowered we feel as well.**

We need to find more ways to empower others and our friends. Nobody deserves to be constantly criticized. They need people like us to help them feel great about themselves.

There is nothing worse than when people constantly criticize what we say or do. I remember going to work on a Monday morning and my boss wanted to have a meeting with me and my co-worker and gave us a strong talking to. He criticized us, and specifically me, for doing a few things wrong and said how bad we were doing. At the end of it all, I said to him, *"Ok, I'll remember that, do you think we can stop now before I feel like total crap, this really isn't a great way to start the week."*

How do you think I did my job for the rest of the day? I was feeling like crap, I wasn't feeling empowered to do a better job, I was feeling inadequate, insecure and I started hating my job and who I was working for.

If he had found a way to tell me what I did wrong and then motivated me, I would have been trying to find ways to do a better job, but instead I walked out of the office with my head hanging low and no energy or desire to work and do a good job.

ACTION STEPS:

Give out more compliments, even to people you don't know – in fact, especially to those you don't know. It really is a special gift to give compliments to friends you haven't met yet (strangers). Write about a person you criticized, how you could have complimented him or her instead of criticizing them.

Find ways to empower people, not criticize them. Find the good in your friends and let them know. Write them a note or give them a call.

SECRET:

Find the good in people, and empower them, don't always look for a reason to criticize someone.

B.C. Fleming is a Facebook friend of mine who is also a fellow burn survivor and speaker. He has an incredible story of being severely injured by the savage attack of a suicide bomber who exploded 3-feet away from him in

Kandahar, Afghanistan on July 24th, 2006. He was also awarded a purple heart in 2010.

Dear Kelly:

My secret: "I know I am here for a reason."

It is often difficult for a person on a mission to care about the minor details and criticisms of others because that person is, many times, so focused on their final goal that everything in their life either falls into its contributing role for the mission at hand or it gets tossed to the wayside because it is not mission essential. The self-esteem of the person on a mission is not determined by what others think of him or her, but by their confidence in their own ability to complete the mission.

When you are narrowly focused on your objective, many obstacles, people, and tragic situations will still stand in your way, but as long as a you know that you are here for a reason, stay focused on the end goal, fear the failure of your mission more than you fear obstacles and the opinions of others, and act according to your convictions, you will have taken the lead in the race. A sense of purpose and an unwillingness to lie down, die, and fail will push you across the finish line. But you must believe you are here for a reason. Otherwise, there would be no purpose for anything and everything would eventually mean nothing and the hope for nothing is self-defeating and doesn't motivate anybody to become better or cause them to believe in themselves.

B.C. Fleming
Author and Speaker
www.BlownUpGuy.com

ക ക ക

Dear Kelly,

My secret to great self-esteem is self-expression. Have you noticed that when you are trying to please others, holding in your feelings, putting up with hurts and not connecting with your spirit then your self-esteem suffers? It doesn't matter what you look like, what you do or what "tricks" you try to build your self-esteem; if you aren't being true to whom you are, the effect will fade.

My passion is for every woman to believe that she is amazing and beautiful just as she is – no changes required. When we can truly believe that and express our uniqueness, life changes completely. No one can destroy your self-esteem when you truly own that statement.

Seem like a big order? It may take some effort to get there and there are many ways to do just that:

- *Do something every day that causes you to be impressed with yourself. Stretch your boundaries.*
- *Accept compliments graciously. You will start to believe them!*
- *Celebrate your successes. Remember to pat yourself on the back for a job well done.*
- *Be present in every moment. Notice your senses. What you experience with your senses – how you receive and give out information - reflects who you are and what's important to you.*
- *Speak your truth. Have the difficult conversations that you've been avoiding.*
- *Learn how to say NO! If something doesn't serve you, don't agree to it.*
- *Take 'me' time every day. You are the most important person in your life.*

Christie Mawer
www.TheBadKitty.com
Best Selling Author
Sensuality Coach

CHAPTER 4

DON'T POSTPONE JOY

"How much of your life are you gonna spend watching everyone else be happy?" ~ *Chad Hymas*

I noticed that when I did things I hated, I started hating my life and ultimately me. There was no way I could feel greater than great because I wasn't doing what I loved to do. When I was fulfilling my passion, everything seemed easy and I could work for 24 hours with no break. I didn't need sleep and I felt energized and empowered. I felt GREAT because I was doing something that was motivating and fulfilling me.

I'm not a morning person and I'm usually late, but when I'm fulfilling my passion and doing what brings me joy, there's nothing that can stop me. I'll be up at 4 am if I need to be. I'll be hours early for a speaking engagement because I love it. It brings me joy knowing that I get the honor of sharing my message with others.

Why do stuff you hate? One time I was approached by a friend to sell life insurance. She thought I was a superstar and that I would be great at it. Are you kidding me? I would suck at it. I wouldn't have been able to get out of bed to go talk to people about life insurance. The idea brought pain to me not joy. I thought there was no way I could take that job; I would not only disappoint my friend but also, myself.

Another time I thought I could be a telemarketer and sell tickets to a dinner theatre that I loved. I thought it would be easy to sell tickets for this dinner theatre, I loved the place, and of course I could sell tickets to it!

Who the heck was I kidding? I hated it! I did it for one day. I couldn't go back the next morning, it gave me pain just thinking about going back to that job.

I don't understand how people think they will be happy and successful doing something they hate.

I feel so bad for people who sell door-to-door. Sometimes you can just tell they hate every minute of what they're doing. You can just feel it in them. They're only doing it because they think they don't have any other option. Someday I want to grab them and say look, quit doing this, it's bringing you pain not joy. Go do your passion in life. Don't postpone joy!

Another example is when I was speaking to a group of teenage girls. I asked if there was anyone who played the piano to put up their hands. Then I said, *"Who hates taking piano lessons?"* A lot of the girls put up their hands. Then I asked, *"How many of you are getting good at it?"* And most of them put their hands back up. *"How about those who love their piano lessons, how many of you are getting good at it?"* and all of them put up their hands.

"Those girls who love their piano lessons, how many hours are they practicing a week? Those who hate it, how many hours are they practicing? Of course, you can't practice more because you hate it! How can you possibly get good and feel good about it if you hate it and don't practice it?"

I believe that if you were doing something you love, you would want to work at it and invest time in it and you would be great at it. Find out what that 'something' is, and do it. Do whatever it is that you love and feel great about. Maybe you don't want to play the piano, but you would love to do something else you are passionate about - do it!

How can you expect to get good at something you hate doing? And if you don't get good at it, what does that do for your self-esteem? Nothing! Zippo! It does nothing to improve your self-esteem, in fact it hurts it.

The reason it hurts your self-esteem is because you are constantly reminding yourself you aren't good at it, because you can't get better at it, because you don't like doing it.

Now, how about when you do something you love and experience joy with? What happens with your self-esteem then? It goes up, right? So again, I ask *why are you doing things that give you pain and not the things that give you joy?* **Joy builds your self-esteem, pain depletes it.**

When I'm doing things I love, I get better at it and when I'm successful, I tell myself how great I am doing and of course it empowers me and boosts my self-esteem.

I felt horrible when my mom made my sister and I take organ lessons. Every week we had to go to lessons and we hated it.

Just before we were supposed to leave for our lessons, my sister and I would start scrambling. We would each take turns getting on the organ and practicing for five-minutes each. We didn't want to get in trouble from our teacher for not practicing. We hated when she asked us if we practiced or not. At least if we practiced before we left, we could say that yes we did practice even though we didn't practice the other six days of the week.

The teacher made us do these little drills over and over a million times and play these songs we hated. We couldn't get out of those lessons fast enough and every time we were finished, we knew we had disappointed our teacher and ourselves and ultimately our mom because we weren't getting any better.

My sister and I were both so relieved when my mom finally realized it was a waste of time and money making us take the organ lessons. You see, her dream was for us to become famous musicians; **her passion, not ours.**

When you do things you love in your life, you become great at them and there's no better way to develop self-esteem than to do things you're good at.

When our Mom put us into horseback riding lessons, we got great at it because every day we were riding our horses. And every riding lesson we had, our teacher saw us improving. How come we couldn't get better at organ lessons, but we could be great at riding horses?

Not because we weren't capable of it, it was because we didn't have the desire to. We had no desire to become famous musicians, but we did have the desire to become fantastic riders and it showed because we improved.

Another example is my dislike for doing bookkeeping. I procrastinate until I'm practically forced to do it. I hate it so much it gives me pain. Just thinking about it makes me ill. But I love typing and I'm great at it. I can type 100 words per minute. If you asked me to type a 100-page report for you, I'd have it done tomorrow.

Wanna hear a funny story? If you asked me to do your bookkeeping, it would take me 10-years to do it and I'm not joking.

What do you think builds my self-esteem - bookkeeping or typing? Because I'm so bad at accounting, it makes me feel horrible - it doesn't build me up, in fact, it drags me down and I feel like a complete loser because I can't find the energy to do it. But, typing makes me feel great. I'm proud that I can type so fast. I can almost type as fast as I can think and I always challenge myself to type faster. I love it! It's one small way that I build my self-esteem.

Of course, you are getting good at the things you love because you focus on them. You find ways to do them more often than the things you hate. You find time to do the things you love and procrastinate about the things you hate.

When I first learned how to scrapbook, you couldn't stop me from doing it, I loved it so much. I found a way to do it every day. I found magazines and courses and learned everything I could. I was fantastic at scrapbooking. It was my passion; I was so passionate about it that I started selling it and teaching others and sharing what I knew.

I was so passionate that I even found a way to make it my business and created a mobile scrapbook store out of a one-tonne cube van. I travelled all over the province and sold supplies and taught people how to scrapbook. I became the scrapbooking queen in my own mind and all my friends knew who to come to when they needed help with their photographs.

My self-esteem grew tremendously because I was doing something I loved. Bookkeeping doesn't do that for me, not at all. Bookkeeping takes away from my self-esteem whereas scrapbooking builds it.

Find things in your life that you love and do them. Sometimes we all have to do things we hate, find a way to ease the pain so you can at least get those things done.

For example, with bookkeeping, the way to ease my pain would be to hire someone who loves to do it and pay them to do it for me. What's great about that is that they can get it done quickly because they love it.

What would take me 20-hours to do will only take them maybe, two. I've noticed that when you love to do something you can get it done more quickly than when you hate it. For someone who hates typing, it might take them 20-hours to type something that would take me two-hours.

The same thing applies to your work or job. When you spend eight-hours a day at a job you hate, you become more miserable. You don't become happier or build your self-esteem; you deplete it, slowly but surely. Then finally one day you say to yourself, what the heck am I doing? Why am I still at this job I hate that it is making me miserable?

I always admired that my grandma started her first job at Eaton's when she was 20-years-old and retired there when she was 65 - 45 years later. I was totally amazed to know someone who could work at the same job for such a long time.

I could never do that. I would be so totally bored to do the same job for 45-years; I would be a dead soul. Physically and emotionally, I couldn't do it. It would do absolutely nothing for me. I couldn't imagine doing the same thing five-days a week, eight-hours a day for 45-years just because my parent or grandparent said you have to get a job and stick with it until you retire at 65-years-old. I don't ever expect to retire. Why would I? If I'm doing something I love, I expect I'll be fulfilling my passion until the day I die.

I loved when I worked for the temporary employment agencies. If I didn't like the job or the company I was working for, I could handle it because I knew that I was only there for a short time. It didn't hurt my self-esteem, in fact it enhanced it. I looked at those assignments as an opportunity to grow. I was able to meet lots of people, be exposed to many different industries, and learned what industries I liked or didn't like.

The biggest bonus was that I developed tremendous computer skills as I was exposed to many different computers and programs. This made me more in demand because I was able to adapt to different companies' needs quickly.

Many times the companies asked for my resume so they could hire me back and if I liked the company I would give them my resume and if I didn't, I wouldn't.

So, my question to you is this, how and why do you stay at a job you hate and makes you miserable when if you did something you loved, you would really enjoy your day and feel great about yourself? I know, a lot of people don't want to give up their pay cheque, but don't you think you'll get a pay cheque at your new job you're passionate about?

Or, if you can't give up your job totally to find a new one, find a way to do your passion even just a little bit in the evenings and weekends. The more you squeeze your passion into your life, the more it will help you to feel happier.

When I decided I wanted to be a professional speaker, I didn't just go and quit my job and freak the family out. I worked at my job full-time and then spent my evenings developing my skills, creating my website, developing my marketing strategy and writing my book. Whenever I had a free minute, I was working on my passion until I decided I was ready to quit my job and be a speaker full-time.

One thing I've learned is that when you follow your passion, the money comes too. It is a known fact that people who spend all day doing jobs they love are happier people and being happy also creates great self-esteem.

For example, let's take Wayne Gretzky, the world's greatest hockey player. When Wayne learned how to skate, his dad couldn't get him off the ice. Wayne was practicing without being told to practice, he loved it so much. He was up and on the rink at 5 a.m. every day and skated for hours and hours at a time.

When Wayne was on the ice, his self-esteem was so tremendous there was no way to knock him down. Fast forward to when Wayne played professional hockey. Wayne's job was to play hockey and lots of it. Not only did he have games, but practices too and he travelled extensively and played as much as he could.

It was very obvious that Wayne's passion was hockey and he loved to go to work every day and as a result became Gretzky the Great, the greatest hockey player in the world. He's broken all the world records in hockey.

Do you think Wayne would be that great if he was a football player? Do you think that if someone said to Wayne, I'll give you twice as much money as you make in hockey and you are going to become the greatest football player in the world instead...

No more hockey for you, it's all about football now. Do you think that he would be just as successful in football as he was in hockey?

Do you think Wayne would have become the greatest football player in the world? No way, his passion was hockey, you wouldn't have been able to get him to a football practice because he would have wanted to play hockey. He wouldn't have been able to visualize himself playing football because he was visualizing himself playing his passion, hockey.

So tell me, why are you doing a job you hate when doing your passion would make you feel great, energized and motivated? **People become great when they're doing things they love; not when they do things they hate.** Think of all the great, successful people you know - are they following their passions? You bet they are. When you follow your passion, you will feel so great and awesome and your self-esteem will explode.

Think of Oprah Winfrey. Do you think she would have become the all-time greatest talk show host in the world if she didn't have a passion for it? She was successful because she followed her passion and only does what she loves.

Following is a chart explaining how doing what you love improves your self-esteem versus doing what you hate. Imagine yourself and what you are doing in your life. Are you doing what you love or hate?

ACTION STEPS:

Write down the things you love to do. Find a minimum of five things. Write down the things you hate to do and find ways that you can eliminate the pain of doing the things you hate.

SECRET:

Do what you love not what you hate.

Dear Kelly,

The secret to my self-esteem is always believing in myself and surrounding myself with positive influences. Even as a small child, I had an innate belief in myself. For as long as I can remember, I have had a rich internal life where I've dreamt of the life that I really wanted to live. I didn't realize it at the time, but I was engaging in positive visualization. My daydreams were so rich that I could actually feel what my life would be like as if my dreams were real. As a result, I've always known that I was capable of being, doing, and receiving more than I currently had and was experiencing, even when others said I couldn't. Seeing and feeling what it was like to live in my dream world helped it come into reality as I grew older.

*I seek out what brings more lightness and happiness into my life. I love spending time with people who are possibility thinkers. Creating a positive environment is so important to me that it inspired me to write a children's book about it, **The Little Rose**. The story is about a little rose who grows up in a weedbed and believes that she is the weed. It empowers children to embrace their differences as unique gifts and to always believe in themselves, despite how others might treat them. **The Little Rose** is a #1 best seller, an incredible dream come true. I'm so happy that my book is making a positive difference in the world.*

The secret of self-esteem is to go deep within and listen to what's right for you, visualize the life you desire, surround yourself with positive environments (people, places, things, and experiences that bring you joy), and take consistent inspired action to pursue your dreams. Act as if your dreams really can come true, because in fact, they will!

Sheri Fink
Author of the #1 Best Selling Children's Book,
The Little Rose
www.SheriFink.com

ஓ ஓ ஓ

Dear Kelly,

I believe the secret to self-esteem is how much you value yourself and how important you think you are. It's how you see yourself and how you feel about your achievements. Self-esteem isn't about bragging about how great and wonderful you are. It's more like quietly knowing that you're worth a tremendous amount. It's not about thinking you're perfect — because nobody is — but knowing that you're worthy of being loved and accepted.

Self-esteem is also not about having only strengths. Your weaknesses, upon self-discovery, become your greatest gift. They teach us a lesson about ourselves. When you learn to embrace your weaknesses, you will turn them into an opportunity, and then begin to discover more about yourself. I believe that self-awareness, then, is the first-step to making that step towards change.

Brynda Roche
www.dynamicyou.nsedreams.com

CHAPTER 5

ASSOCIATE WITH EMPOWERING PEOPLE AND DEVELOP CHAMPIONS AND MENTORS IN YOUR LIFE

"No pessimist ever discovered the secrets of the stars, or sailed to an uncharted land, or opened a new heaven to the human spirit." ~ Helen Keller

The Christmas when I was writing my book *'No Risk No Rewards,'* a friend and mentor, Darren Jacklin came over because he needed some help from me. We got talking about the projects we were working on and how we were helping people and having a great conversation. What we thought was going to be a short half hour visit, ended up being a two-hour visit and Darren staying for supper. When he left, I was full of this incredible energy and motivation and I just had to write more in my book. I had even more ideas to add.

The next day I called another friend and she came over and we started talking about all the things she was doing and again, I felt this incredible energy and motivation.

Then another time I talked to a friend who wasn't following her passion and she was questioning what I was doing and trying to make me doubt myself and my abilities and then I started thinking, what is going on?

Why is it that when I talk with certain friends, I feel great about myself and when I talk to other friends, I feel crappy? Which are the right friends for me? Who is going to help me grow and prosper? Who is going to help me with my self-esteem and who is going to try and steer me off course? Who do I have time for and who should I make time for? I also began realizing my true support of friends/family.

I remember Darren telling me the story of his friend who called him up in a depressed mood and wanted Darren to motivate him so he could get out of his funk and no matter what Darren said, the guy didn't want to do it. He had excuse after excuse as to why he couldn't do it. Finally, Darren couldn't help him at all - this guy didn't really want to be helped and without knowing it, he tried to suck the life out of Darren.

He found it hard to believe how Darren could be so positive about life, when he felt like crap. The next time he called Darren, Darren had no time for him. He became a distraction to Darren at that time of day. Darren needed an enhancement so he could keep himself motivated and empowered. Darren actually told him, *"Sorry, I can't talk to you; you're a distraction in my life who doesn't want to be helped. I need positive influences in my life and you're not one of them."*

So, do your friends enhance your life or distract your life? I find that I need friends who enhance my life, empower me and help me to stay on the right track, not the friends who try to distract me and create self-doubt for me.

For example, if I was to phone Darren and say, *"Hey Darren, guess what, I'm starting to write my next book called Self-esteem Doesn't Come in a Bottle."* What do you think Darren would say?

I think he would say, *"Wow, how awesome Kel, I love hearing how you're taking consistent action towards your passion and helping others along the way."* Another friend/mentor Bob Hooey said, *"Wow Kel, love it, what can I do to help?"*

If I was to phone my negative friend and say the same thing, she would say, "*Wow, really, already? How are you going to do that? Seriously?*"

Who do you think I should listen to? Who is going to give me the encouragement I need to finish and market this book? By the way, Darren actually did say what I thought he would say.

Another example is when I talked to a friend about my becoming a speaker. She kept telling me how being a speaker is a tough world to break into and how there's so many speakers out there who aren't making money and how the recession really hurt a lot of speakers; generally trying to discourage me from following my passion of being a speaker. Her final words were, "*Don't let me discourage you from being a speaker; I just want you to know it's a tough world out there.*"

Wow, was that empowering or what? I was so scared of being a speaker and failing, I didn't know what to do.

Then I talked to my champion Jack Zufelt (who also wrote the foreword to my book '*No Risk No Rewards*') and told him about my desire to be a speaker and how whenever I speak, I get this incredible feeling in my heart and this vibration that just makes me want to speak more and more, and how gratifying and humble I feel. Jack said, "*Kelly that is your core desire, your passion. You are following your core desire and you need to keep doing it. You can't stop; you need to share your story with the world because you can help so many people with your story. What can I do to help you?*"

Wow, what a difference. Who do you think I listened to? My friend who was trying to talk me out of my passion or my mentor who was trying to encourage me to follow my passion and help others?

I'll tell you what - I'm so glad I listened to Jack. I've been speaking ever since and I get these wonderful emails from people who tell me how much my story helped them. If I would have listened to my negative friend, I wouldn't be speaking, because it's a tough world out there, don't you know?

Since I've been following my passion, it hasn't been a tough world - it's been an easy world. It's been very humbling sharing my story and learning that I truly can help other people. People are calling or emailing me all the time asking if I'll speak for them or if they can write a story about me or blog about me. People want to help because they love my message and if a burn survivor can do it, so can you.

You just have to believe in yourself and not let other people's beliefs stop you. What I love about other people helping me is that I'm also helping them and all their readers and viewers. Together we are sharing my message that beauty comes from the heart and together we are helping to inspire others.

I love when a blogger says to me, "*I think my readers would love your story and you can help them.*" I always say, "*Absolutely, let's do it, you never know what message people are going to get and I just want people to feel great about themselves.*"

Why have Champions and Mentors in your life?

I am a very big believer in champions and mentors. I honestly don't know if I would be a speaker or author without them. Whenever I'm confused about something or need some inspiration or even need a good kick in the butt, they are who I call.

I would never call a negative friend if I needed inspiration because that friend would bring me down to their level instead of empower and inspire me. That is the absolutely wrong thing to do. Negative people love when you accept that you really can't do something that you knew you could do. So I call my champions and mentors. They are fabulous.

What is a Champion?

A champion is someone who knows you very well, empowers you and champions you to others. Your champion is someone who you can go to and will give you the honest truth about what you need to do. You can tell them anything and they know how to motivate you to get the job done. A true champion is someone who stands behind you and is not scared to tell you what they think. They empower you to be the very best you can be and they find things inside you that you didn't know you had.

Your champion is the person you go to when you're feeling insecure and you need that one person to pick you up, dust you off, wind you up and make you go again. They are the one person who doesn't forget how awesome you are and knows how to make you feel great about yourself again. They also always remind me of my purpose in my life.

They guide me and help me make decisions based on me achieving my goals, not failing at my goals. They know my vision and passion and where I want to go in life. They help me to see that my dreams are real and can be accomplished.

I have different champions and mentors for every area of my life. I have speaking champions like Charmaine Hammond, Cheryl Cran, Bob Hooey and Jack Zufelt. My speaking champions are speakers themselves and then I have two other champions who aren't speakers, but know me more spiritually and they help in those areas. You must have champions in your own industry because they've done it; they're already successful and know what it takes to help you get there too.

What is a Mentor?

Mentors are also important, they are like coaches. A mentor offers you support, guidance and assistance to help you work through your problems and challenges in your business and/or personal life. Don't be shy about asking someone to be your mentor or champion. True mentors and champions love being asked, it makes them feel honored and proud that you want to learn from them.

ACTION STEPS:

Make a list of people who inspire you and find ways to keep in touch with them.

Sign up for www.tut.com – every day you will get inspiring emails from the universe that will help you to keep you motivated.

Find ways to minimize the amount of interaction you have with the negative people in your life. Determine who is a champion and a mentor in your life and who can help you to *succeed* to the fullest!

SECRET:

Connect with people who inspire and empower you and learn from them.

Dear Kelly:

Here's my "secret." Every religion, successful person, philosopher, athlete etc. share the same simple belief "thoughts become things." Your thoughts are determined by what you ALLOW to come into your reality. If you can control what you put in, you can control what comes out. It boils down to the people you spend the majority of your time with, the books you read (study and apply), and the audio you listen to.

I am forced to have a great self-image and positive attitude because I spend my time with great people. Most of my waking moments are spent with my girlfriend Jessica, Napoleon Hill, Jay Z, John

Maxwell and my business mentors. I read my goals and surround myself visually with what I intend my life to look like. "Magically" all those things produce themselves in my reality. What goes in my mind and I choose to focus on will EVENTUALLY come to fruition.

Jeff Samis
www.JeffSamis.com

෪ ෪ ෪

Dear Kelly,

The secret to my self-esteem is knowing that I am not my job, career accomplishments, academic qualifications, or life roles (wife, sister, daughter, friend, coach or colleague).

It is being clear about my highest values: integrity, compassion and courage. It is daily meditation where I find and meet me and God the Source of my inner strength. And that is where I am reminded that I am love and self-acceptance.

Dr Lorwai TAN PhD
Financial Freedom Fighter
http://yourmoneyandyourmindset.com

෪ ෪ ෪

Dear Kelly,

The secret to my self-esteem is asking myself, "What voice within my mind am I open to listening to today?" I suffered from low self-esteem my whole life. From being on welfare, drug and alcohol addiction, depression and abusive relationships I never imagined life could be anything more.

Before my spiritual awakening, the only voice in my head I listened to was that of my inner critic, the fearful or doubtful self. Disciplining myself to sit in silence and meditate each day turned my life around. I began to hear another voice, the voice of my Higher Self or what I now refer to as my Brilliant Self. The more I meditated, the more I discovered how to connect to this deeper part of me that was wise, loving and always spoke truth. My Brilliant Self always assures me that I am on the right path and that no matter what choice I make, it is the right choice for there are many lessons in all I choose.

The biggest insight for me in experiencing a higher level of self-esteem was discovering that I no longer had to believe in my inner

52

critic when it showed up. I could now just listen, let it rant, and in becoming the observer of my own thoughts, I was able to disconnect from the fear and doubt. I then realized these parts of me existed as long as I ignored or avoided them. The more I began to acknowledge my fear and appreciate its existence the negative energy began to dissolve and in its place was peace of mind.

We can either tune into the voice of the inner critic or we can tune into the loving voice of our Brilliant Self that is always guiding us to open our hearts especially to our SELVES. For Self Love is the key to a higher level of self-respect.

Karen Klassen
Founder of Women Embracing Brilliance.
www.womenembracingbrilliance.com

ॐ ॐ ॐ

Dear Kelly,

My secret to self-esteem is when I feel, I feel! That is, when I feel rather than think about being the best for the world, I experience a WELLthier sense of who I am. After all, I'm a feeling person thinking!

Yes = WELLthier = based on WELLth = well-being to the nth degree

Cheers,
Stephen Hobbs, EdD
www.WELLThLearning.com
www.ManagingLeading.com

CHAPTER 6

LEARN HOW TO LAUGH AT YOURSELF

This chapter is dedicated to two of my oldest friends Paul Edwards and Cindy Mitchell. I'll never forget the day I met Paul. I was in grade four and he was in grade five, and we were both members of the school library audio visual club. That meant we got to go to the classrooms and set up the movie projectors.

Paul was the President of the club and called a meeting so we could all meet and he could teach us how to operate the equipment. At the meeting he says, *"Kelly, you're Kelly?"* and I said *"Yes, I'm Kelly."* And then Paul says, *"Well, I thought you'd be a boy Kelly not a girl Kelly."* *"When I saw your name on the list I just assumed you were a boy Kelly."* We both laughed; he broke the ice and we have been friends ever since. In high school, we became even better friends and he was even my date for my grade 12 graduation.

One of my funniest memories was when Paul had to have his jaw broken and wired shut for six weeks. My best friend and her boyfriend and I went over to Paul's house to hang out. Paul's mom invited us over because Paul didn't want to go out with his mouth wired and she thought he needed some cheering up.

We had a great time hanging out together even though Paul couldn't talk. Paul's parents had just bought a brand new computer which was so amazing because that's when computers were just coming out and he was showing me how to play a game. I sucked so bad at it and Paul had to keep taking over for me because I just couldn't make that little computer guy jump. It was so hard for him because he couldn't tell me how to do it, he had to show me and then when I couldn't do it, he couldn't laugh at me, only grunt. Ok, hold it – maybe that was a good thing he couldn't laugh at me. Hehe

Then Paul's mom came upstairs and I don't know how it happened but she asked if she could play with my hair. She said her daughter never lets her, but she would really love to. So I said *"Sure, go ahead Mrs. Edwards, you can do whatever you want, I'll just sit here."*

She took a curling iron, a brush and comb and away she went. She was doing all kinds of stuff to my hair. She was having fun and when she finally came up with her final funky hairstyle for me, she turned to my best friend and said, *"Well, what do you think?"* My best friend had just finished her hair dressing training in school and said, *"Well, I think you could do this and this instead, it really is kind of weird."* And she quietly said to me, *"Kel I can't believe you're letting her do this to you."* I just shrugged my shoulders and said *"Why not? She's having fun, it's just hair and it's not permanent."* And then I said to Mrs. Edwards, *"I think it looks great."*

And then, Mrs. Edwards did what we all knew she would do, but were regretting, she turned to her son Paul and said, *"Paulie, doesn't Kelly look beautiful like this?"* I just laughed, poor Paul's mouth was wired shut and he couldn't say anything and it was probably a good thing because she really put him on the spot.

I know he didn't want to hurt his mom's feelings or mine so I think he lucked out on that one and was glad his mouth was wired shut. I have no clue what he would have said if he could have, but I was just thankful that he couldn't say anything. Poor Paul. I laughed and said to him, *"It's ok Paul, I'm having fun here with your mom, she's doing a great job no matter what anyone thinks."*

You see, Paul has this crazy sense of humor that I love (and Cindy too). This is one person who I have never seen get mad. He always finds a way to bring humor in his life and whenever I'm around him, he always makes me feel special, even when I'm feeling pretty crappy. He has this amazing gift that makes everyone feel great around him and no one is ever left out.

Paul was recently promoted to Vice President of Air Liquide Canada, a worldwide medical gas company that helps people with chronic breathing diseases; and because of the promotion had to move to Ontario.

At Paul and Cindy's going away party, he was telling me the story of a half marathon he ran and how he did soooooo well that he got passed by a guy in a wheelchair - not once, but twice! Twice he got passed by the guy in the wheel chair and it gets better! The guy's wheel even fell off and had to be fixed and he still beat Paul. We couldn't stop laughing at the story.

Paul thought it was so funny that he got passed twice by the guy in the wheelchair. He wasn't mad at himself for not winning the race; he took the situation and made it a happy one for himself. He found a way to laugh at himself; not be embarrassed by it. You see, what I love is when we can laugh at ourselves. We need to learn how to laugh more in life. Life doesn't have to be so serious all the time. Life has to be fun - if it isn't, why are we in it?

For example, one of my recent laughs is the winter of 2010. It was the worst winter ever; snow was two miles high and we were colder than all the deep freezers put together. Worst winter ever and I was majorly miserable. I was even miserable in October before the snow started flying because somehow I just knew it was going to be a very long and very cold winter.

One morning, I had to drive to work and I'm backing up my mini-van (or at least trying to back up). My poor old mini-van didn't want to do anything, I at least got to sleep in a warm house, my mini-van had to suffer outside in the cold bitter wind and let snow fall on it. And the snow was a foot high on the roof and I'm totally serious.

It took everything my poor mini-van had to back up, and I was thinking - *oh no, my poor van doesn't want to go, it's sooooo cold, no, it's FREEZING! I don't blame it.* My minivan was colder than cold and making some very loud screaming noises! Eventually it backed up and when I put it in drive to go forward, I heard the very loud clunking noises. My poor van didn't want to go forward either. If I thought going in reverse was bad, forward was worse! No matter how much I pushed on the gas, it wasn't going ahead.

I thought oh no, the transmission is finally gone and so I backed my van up back into my driveway and I called my husband Max and said *"Ok, I think I finally did it, the transmission is gone, it's making these really loud clunking noises and it doesn't want to go forward or reverse."*

My mini-van was nine-years-old and had 280,000 kilometres on it and so we were expecting it to die soon. We were both upset because I really didn't want to buy anything at that time. I wanted to go another year without car payments. Max was at work and he started looking at second hand vehicles for me and even texted some pictures of some for me. I was getting madder because it really wasn't a good time to buy something else and I just wanted to avoid the situation.

Max came home from work so that he could have a look at the van and see if it really was the transmission. He came into the house and said *"You know you have a flat tire don't you?"* And I said *"No way, flat tires don't make that kind of clunking sound."* And he said, *"Oh yes they do, when they're that flat and frozen to the driveway."* And sure enough, all I had was a flat tire. The transmission was fine and he even took it to a mechanic to get it checked out.

Well, all I could do was laugh. What a goof I was, how could I not notice the flat tire? Max said, *"You are not putting this on Facebook, I'm embarrassed to call you my wife right now."* And I of course said *"Why not? Whatever, it's just a flat tire. LOL LOL"*

I had already put on Facebook that I was worried the clunking meant I had finally killed off my old van that I swore I would drive until it was dead. Yeah I was just a little embarrassed that it was just a flat tire, but so what, who cares?

I'm a gal who loves to have fun and so what if I laugh at myself. If I can't laugh at me, who can?

I will never forget one of my most embarrassing moments in my whole life. I was President of the Alberta Burn Rehabilitation Society at the time and I was only 21-years-old. I was stepping down from Presidency and we were having our annual board meeting. I was telling them that I wasn't running again and they pleaded with me to do it one more year. They promised to give me more help.

The room was full of doctors, nurses, firefighters and other members. All of a sudden, the room was totally quiet and I farted and it sounded like a perfect little TOOT. I was shocked and didn't know if anyone heard it. I'm half deaf, so I know most people can hear a thousand times better than me, so there was a faint chance that someone could have heard it. Or maybe not. I kept thinking to myself did anyone hear it? Oh no, what should I do? Everyone was looking around at each other, not knowing what to do. Those 10-seconds seemed like 10-minutes in my head.

I couldn't hold it in any longer and I burst out laughing. Then everyone else started laughing too. In fact we were all laughing so hard we were crying. There was nothing else to do. I could have pretended it didn't happen or run out of the room crying of embarrassment or something silly like that, but no, I laughed and everyone else laughed with me.

It was a perfect little toot, nobody can fart like that! It sounded funny and so we all laughed and it broke the tension and we enjoyed the moment. I laughed, they laughed, we all had a great laugh. They didn't think any less of me, they were proud that I could laugh at myself. And no, it didn't make me stay on as president, I still resigned. They were probably glad it was me that farted and not them. I don't know if anybody else would have handled the situation like I did, but it seemed like the best thing to do at the time.

ACTION STEPS:

Write down instances that you laughed at yourself. Also write down times when you got mad when you really could have laughed.

SECRET:

The more reasons you find to laugh, the happier you will be.

Dear Kelly:

To me, great self-esteem comes with a peaceful inner knowing of who I am and what my purpose is here on earth. Working with that insight allows me to recognize no one is like me and yet we are all the same.

Every day brings about new learning and growing opportunities. How we handle those opportunities makes a huge difference.

I come from a place of having the awareness that the messengers around me potentially have messages for me. What I do with those messages is what helps me to feel the peace within myself. The Universe aligns everything in my life in divine perfection. I'm grateful for this realization of the perfection as it allows me to truly know myself.

Sheila Unique
...clearing paths to Self Empowerment
...an Intuitive who discovers your Unique Self!
www.UniqueEnergy.ca

₡ ₡ ₡

Dear Kelly,

When you asked me to give my secret to self-esteem, it made me think because I've never thought about it before. After briefly thinking about it, the answer was clear and here it is. "Hope you're ready for this breaking news that's going to change the course of the world." LOL (LOL means 'laughing out loud')

The secret to my self-esteem is me recognizing that it's not about me. It's me realizing that people care way less about me than what I thought. **People care about their wants, their needs, their passions, their pains, not about what you look like or about what you have or don't have.**

Once I realized this, I started living my life on my terms. The result of this realization is me now having a strong sense of self, living in monument, and not worrying about what people may or may not think of me. I'm now able to live powerfully and create new possibilities for myself and create a world I love "from scratch."

Eric A Billie Kai-Lewis
www.new-billionaires.com
www.createmarketingsystem.com

Dear Kelly:

My secret to self-esteem: Well that took me over 40 years to realize and I still work on it daily. We are all unique, imperfect human beings and the sooner we love ourselves and accept ourselves with that as our mantra, the better the world will be. The best advice I was ever given, was to focus on my strengths, and not my weaknesses. When I did that, I began to realize I had many strengths and began to laugh about my weaknesses. We all have both and the choice is about where we want to spend our precious time and energy. A very wise person gave me a gift that had an engraving on it that said:

Watch your thoughts, for they become words. Choose your words, for they become actions. Understand your actions, for they become habits. Study your habits, for they become your character. Develop your character for it becomes your destiny.

Dianna Bowes
www.fabulousat50.com

ⅎ ⅎ ⅎ

Dear Kelly,

When you asked me that question, "Where did I get my self-confidence," I had to think hard on that. It's probably because I had the guts to go for something I believed in and then felt proud of myself at how well it turned out. Also realizing I didn't give up even though the odds were not in my favor. You do that a couple of times and you start to feel and believe you can do anything. I also do not let little issues get to me.

That's probably a result of self-confidence. That's certainly a BIG question you asked and I hope I gave you a suitable answer. Keep up your great work, telling people what you're made of. You're a doll!

Dorothy Briggs
www.womanition.com
www.vavasaur.com

CHAPTER 7

SMILE AND SMILE SOME MORE

"Everything has its beauty but not everyone sees it."
~ Confucius

When people first see me, they know I'm different. Sometimes they know I'm burnt but other times they're not sure and they don't know how to treat me. They aren't sure if I'm a happy person or a sad, bitter, insecure burn victim.

When I smile, all of a sudden the ice is broken, and then I seem approachable. I don't seem so scary with all the scars; in fact I seem normal. Many people tell me that when they first meet me they see my scars, but within five-minutes, they forget all about them and they don't ever notice my scars again.

I have gotten in the habit of smiling whenever someone looks at me, even people I don't know. When I smile, it puts me in a good mood plus it makes me seem happier.

People are very quick to judge someone by the expression on their face. If you see someone for the first time and they have a scowl on their face, it's only natural to think that that person is angry, mean or unapproachable. And when you have to deal with that person, you tend to act a little reserved and with caution. The energy is different.

When I'm happy and smiling at people and treat them with respect and like we're friends, then they treat me the same way. They want to help you and it's a great feeling to walk out the door knowing that you made someone feel great and not like crap.

I don't even care if you're a homeless person or a filthy rich person, I smile. Everyone deserves a smile.

One of my favorite songs is "Smile" by Uncle Kracker. It always makes me think of a few certain friends, who I just love, and of course it brings lots of smiles to my face and I'm in my Happy Land all day.

Yes, that's right, I have my own little Happy Land and whenever I get annoyed or upset about something, I think of my Happy Land and then the annoying thing seems to go away. One time I was asked, *"What is with that big grin?"* And I said, *"Oh, I'm in my Happy Land, no need to be upset about anything just be happy."*

What is Happy Land for me? It's all those special places or incidences that happen to me that make me smile. I replay them in my head to make me happy. I know, I sound crazy, but it works. I visualize those little happy scenes in my head over and over and they're great little reminders of how I do have happiness in my life.

If I was to visualize and replay all the crap and things that make me mad, then I just get madder, so I choose to replay the happy stuff instead. Think about when something made you mad. Did you recognize that every time you replayed the situation in your head that you got madder instead of happier?

Exactly! That's my point, so why replay the crap when you can replay the happy stuff instead?

For example, one night I had a discussion with a friend about an incident that made me mad. And then when I went to bed that night, I laid awake for three-hours getting madder and madder and every mad thought I had led to another mad thought and my mind was full of everything that made me mad in my life. It brought my energy to a different level and I didn't like it and I couldn't sleep at all. And then I got mad because I couldn't sleep, but my head was so full of mad thoughts, I couldn't sleep. I was so full of negative energy.

I have learned that when something makes you mad you need to "**Deal with it and Drop it!**"

For example, the other day I was in a situation that really annoyed me and I spent some time thinking about it and thought of different ways I could deal with it. So I dealt with the situation and it was over and done with. So, I followed my policy of Deal with it and Drop it and moved on.

But then the next day, I was driving on our holidays and thought about the situation again and it was making me mad again and then I reminded myself, *hey, you already dealt with it and dropped it, move on and go back to Happy Land where it's more fun!*

People always ask me how I stay calm or how I feel great or how I seem to let the little things just slide away. It's because I play happy scenes and conversations in my head all the time. I find ways to be happy and not sad. I choose to be happy.

If I spend all my time being mad about things, then I have no room for the happy things that are going on in my life. It's one of the biggest reasons that I listen to upbeat, energizing songs and not sad ones.

When I am in an 'off' mood, the last thing I need is to listen to sad songs - I just get sadder! When I need some motivation to get up off the couch, somehow I find a way to listen to fast, upbeat songs, like Smile by Uncle Kracker or I Gotta Feeling by Black Eyed Peas; anything but sad songs. If I need energy, I need to listen to energetic songs.

I can listen to I Gotta Feeling two or three times in a row and by the third time I am off my chair dancing like a crazy fool. Serious. Maybe it's a song that takes you to your Happy Land or maybe it's a visual of someone giving you a compliment or maybe it's a conversation you had with a great friend. Whatever it is, keep replaying your happy thoughts to keep you in your Happy Land.

Just before I get on stage, do you think I'd be able to do a great presentation if I was thinking mad negative thoughts? Absolutely not. In fact, if Alex my daughter comes with me, I now have a rule about her music.

I noticed that as we were driving, her music was making me angry and annoyed and there's no way I can be my happy self if I listen to her music before I get on stage, I need to listen to my music that makes me feel great and empowered. So the rule is that while we're driving on the way to an event, we listen to my music so I can prepare myself mentally. On the way back, she can pick whatever she wants.

ACTION STEPS:

Listen to three sad songs and see how you feel. Now listen to three high energy songs and see how you feel. Which songs make you feel motivated and energized to fulfill your passions in life? Which songs make you feel great?

Make a list of a minimum of five songs that make you the happiest and listen to them as often as you can.

SECRET:

Smile as much as you can and find your Happy Land and replay the happy visuals over and over.

Dear Kelly:

My secret to great self-esteem is that I make a conscious effort every day to smile at the people passing by me, and to offer kinds words. Being kind is something that always makes me feel like I'm a person of substance, no matter what other down faults I may discover within myself.

Denise Beaupre

ॐ ॐ ॐ

Dear Kelly,

The secret to my self-esteem originally stemmed from my loving and nurturing mother. Sadly, she died when I was 10. Since that time I have always been searching for female role models to emulate. I have been lucky to have found both women role models and friends who have supported me, believed in me, and taught me many things as I walk through each day of my life.

I knew that it was important to get educated. I went to college. Next, I went to graduate school and got a PhD in clinical psychology. I was always very ambitious. I guess to this day I always think "Would my mother be proud?" before I do anything. If the answer is yes, then I proceed, full throttle ahead. This year I co-authored a book called Teenage as a Second Language-A Parent's Guide to Becoming Bilingual (Adams Media). I am also the co-creator of an interactive website called talkingteenage.com.

I was then asked to be a parenting expert for Galtime.com and now I'm The Teen Doctor for Psychology Today. So, yes I am thankful for good self-esteem. I owe that to all of the friends and role models who have been there for me.

Barbara Greenberg PhD
www.talkingteenage.com

ॐ ॐ ॐ

Dear Kelly,

A person's self-esteem or belief of their self-worth is one of the biggest beliefs that can have the most significant impact or our challenges or successes. The great news is that we are in control of it as it comes from within us.

While going through my life, I had to realize, accept and honor that what your version of my story is your version and my version is mine. They will never be the same. You will never truly know all the events and the feelings that go with whatever has happened. I do know and I come to terms and accept all of it. I have never let anyone tell me I cannot succeed and live to actually see their stories come to fruition.

The secret is hold your head high and believe what you know in your heart to be true. YOU must love YOU after all, no one else matters. When you start trash talking in your head about yourself, you tell that voice to book an appointment. Remember it has had a lot of experience in not booking appointments. Be tough with it.

We are all beautiful creatures who have been placed on this earth to do one job or another; figure out what job you are passionate about and go about your business of doing it without letting others' beliefs stand in your way. You will be glad you did.

The world is an open road, only you can chose which one you will travel on with your head high!

Shelley Streit
www.guidinglightfinancial

CHAPTER 8

REALIZE EVEN THE WEEDS ARE BEAUTIFUL

*"What makes me feel beautiful is living for me, not trying
to feel beautiful for others, scars and all"*
~ Kelly Falardeau

The title of this chapter was a friendly battle with my friend Dawn Ofner. She and I have known each other since we were 10-years-old and we spend lots of time laughing about things. When I told her about this title, she wanted me to call this chapter 'dandelions are beautiful too'.

She didn't want me to call myself a weed and I didn't want to call myself a dandelion. Weeds are strong, hard to kill and they're different and they stand out amongst the crowd. Fortunately, since I'm the writer, I get to win this one. *I won this one Dawn; you can win all the next friendly battles.* Hehe

I really love the story about how this title came up. I was texting my best friend and he was telling me he was weeding and getting a little annoyed because the weeds always grew the fastest and they never stopped growing. He always had to weed (he's a very avid gardener). I texted him back and said, *"Well, you know, even the weeds are beautiful too."* He texted back and said, *"Yes I guess you're right."*

For some reason, we don't always find the beauty in a weed. We're very quick to just judge it and call it ugly, just because it's a weed.

One day I found this giant exploded dandelion beside my house; it was huge! I had never seen a giant dandelion like this, it took two hands to cover how big and round it was and it was gorgeous. I got my camera and took some amazing pictures of it.

While I was staring at it, I thought wow, I'm supposed to hate this beautiful weed, but I don't, it's gorgeous. At this moment, it's the most gorgeous flower. And yes, I called it a flower because ultimately it is that. It has the same qualities as a flower so why shouldn't it be called a flower?

A dandelion starts out as a simple yellow flower and then it explodes into a ball of white fluff, much like how a plain, simple moth turns into a beautiful butterfly. But why can't it be beautiful? Why do we condition ourselves and kids to believe that simple yellow flowers are ugly weeds?

It's really not about the outer looks; it's the heart and soul that makes a person beautiful. You could have the most gorgeous outer looks in the world and still be considered ugly; much like you can have the ugliest outer looks in the world and still be beautiful.

I bet there's even people in this world who have looked at me and said, "*Wow, is she ever ugly.*" And then I also believe that there's people who think "*Wow, she's gorgeous even with those scars on her face.*" And that's why I believe that other people's opinions don't count and I shouldn't rely on what other people think of my looks in order to dictate what I feel.

For example, as a kid growing up, I devised a beauty scale. I categorized people and gave them a number as to how good looking or ugly I thought they were. The bottom of the scale was homely, then ugly (which is where I ranked myself), ok looking, good looking, beautiful, gorgeous, drop dead gorgeous, hot, and finally, certainly not last, sexy.

Once I categorized you in one of the above categories, I gave you a number and ranked you there also. It was a crazy and stupid system.

I was at the bottom of the pile, how could I make my way to the top or even the middle? As far as I was concerned, I couldn't. There was nothing I could do to get there. I knew my scars would never disappear and I believed at the time that I could only be considered beautiful if I was scarless. I thought I would always be at the bottom of the beauty scale.

The day I truly felt beautiful was the day I quit caring about other people's opinions and whether they thought I was beautiful or not. It just didn't matter. I don't have to be the most beautiful woman in the world according to other people. I don't have to compete with them.

When I became an adult and realized that my beauty scale sucked and did nothing to help me, I stopped it. I stopped rating other people and just accepted that ***I'm the most beautiful woman to me***.

I deserve to feel beautiful and my beauty doesn't have to be rated or compared to any other woman. People's opinions just don't matter to me and I came up with a quote that says:

"Your opinion of me isn't going to change my opinion of me."

I'm me, beautiful me. Scars and all.

Have you ever thought of how animals react when they meet other animals for the first time? Do you think when a dog sees another dog that he's looking at it and thinking, *"Wow, is that ever an ugly mutt, I don't want to associate with him?"* Nope, it would be funny if he did though.

That is the one thing I love about animals, they never judge another animal or person by their looks. They don't care if you're ugly or beautiful. They don't care if you have scars, or if you're fat or if you've got the biggest nose in the world, they just don't care. If you show them love, they will love you right back. They never judge the book by its cover! They might judge the dog by their smell, but it's never about their looks. Did I really say that out loud? That's funny.

ACTION STEPS:

Find something you think is ugly and think of a way to make it seem beautiful? Think of a person you think is ugly and try and find a way to make that person seem beautiful.

SECRET:

Be like animals and try not to judge the book by the cover.

Dear Kelly,

When I need a boost in self-esteem, I go through a 3-step process:

1. If I am feeling bad because I LET others dictate my life, I realize that their opinions don't matter as long as I am doing what is right and true.

2. I open my Bible and read about the "ordinary" people who have done extraordinary things with God's help. I then remember my purpose—that I was designed and created for great things. I know that I am perfect in HIS sight, and as long as I am living my life in the calling that He and I have set before me... all is well.

3. I pray to God to help me see the truth. I pray for those who try to categorize me in the "box" of their lives. I FORGIVE them because I realize they must feel pretty bad about themselves and their lives (even more than I do!).

Kathleen D. Mailer
Author and Founder/Editor-in-Chief
Today's Businesswoman magazine
www.kathleenmailer.com

Dear Kelly,

I believe we are all born with abundant self-esteem from birth. But for the 30-years I lived my life as a perfectionist, my "from birth" esteem was marred by more self-doubt, worry, hurt and guilt than I'd ever let on. To the outside world, I may have seemed a successful overachiever, not affected by anything that ever "happened" to me - we all have our stories. I pretended I'd never been hurt, I pretended all my decisions were good decisions, and I pretended my failures didn't ever happen. I pretended I didn't need love and I pretended I didn't need help. When I was a perfectionist, I believed what I told others and I faked my way to happy.

The moment I became a mother was the moment my perfect facade crumbled. The challenge of keeping it together as a first-time mom was unlike anything I'd faced, and I gave in quickly to imperfection. Because it was simply the only option I had. As two more babies arrived, and I started my businesses, I started to embrace "imperfect" as the path to feeling free! And sharing how imperfect I actually am became extremely cathartic! When I became imperfect, I confronted some old hurts with ease and forgave myself with greater kindness. When I became imperfect, I let my family and friends love me better.

My secret to self-esteem is reminding myself and others that true happiness lies in allowing oneself to be perfectly imperfect.

Kim Page Gluckie
www.iampte.com
www.mpoweredmarketing.com/

CHAPTER 9

FOLLOW THE LAW OF RECIPROCATION

Beauty is infectious. If you radiate beauty through your attitude and spirit, others will feel beautiful too.
~ *Unknown*

It took me a long time to learn this but, there's no reason I should be jealous of someone else's beauty, success, or accomplishments. The universe is full of abundance and there can be many beautiful people - in fact the world is so full of abundance that everyone can be beautiful or successful if they want.

The more we empower others and help them to feel great about themselves, the more empowered we feel ourselves. For example, Troy Payne, a speaker who is a friend of mine, was launching a bestseller campaign for his new book called *'The Road to Resiliency.'* He has an incredible story and was destined to end up dead if he continued on the path he was headed; he even ended up homeless for a period of time. But something changed for him and now he has a rock band and he inspires kids through his music. I love his message and that he's inspiring kids all over the world. An incredible message and an incredible way of doing it. Kids love music and of course they're going to love listening to him.

Essentially Troy and I are both trying to reach the same audience of people, and I could be jealous, but I'm not. Troy asked me if I would help him with his bestseller campaign and of course I said yes and you know why?

By empowering Troy and helping him to be successful, I'm also helping myself too. I feel great helping Troy; I want him to be successful. I want him to be inspiring kids to stay off the streets and off drugs. I want kids to know that even if they are struggling with an addiction that there is hope for them. The world is full of abundance and the kids need his message AND my message.

They need his message because it will give them hope that anyone can take a bad situation and make it good, and they need my message that self-esteem doesn't come in a bottle. There is no way the universe is going to let just one of us succeed; we are both going to succeed.

When I help Troy succeed, naturally he's going to want to help me with my bestseller campaign. In fact, he's already offered and said he can't wait to help me succeed too. It's called the Law of Reciprocation. If you help others to succeed, then you will receive success too.

If you want to feel great about yourself, then help others to feel great about themselves. **Whatever you put out to help others, you will receive back.** It took me a long time to realize that, but it is definitely working.

My Popa (grandpa) taught me two things – always treat others as you would have them treat you and secondly, never say anything you may regret later.

Another example is my friend Amanda Welliver. She has an amazing self-esteem program for youth. I love what she does. She has a speech impediment and grew up in a horrible family environment. I couldn't imagine a mother treating her child the way Amanda's mom treated her. Amanda found a way to take her life experiences and help others.

When she and I first met, I could tell she was feeling a little awkward, but we were just getting to know each other. We got together in person and chatted some more. One day she put on Facebook that she knew of some kids who were graduating and didn't have grad dresses and could anyone help. I had a bridesmaid dress and my wedding dress that were sitting in my closet collecting dust, why not help some young girl to have a beautiful dress to wear? I offered to help and Amanda came over to pick up the dress.

We got talking again and we hit it off and had a great time and tapped into each other's sense of humor. I could tell she was being a little reserved, but couldn't put my finger on it. The next time we got together, it was like we had been friends forever. We were laughing and teasing each other (in a good way of course) and then she proceeded to tell me that when she first met me, she was a little concerned and felt a little threatened by me. She was concerned about whether I was a competitor or not since we were both going after the same market - teenagers and self-esteem.

When she told me that, I said, *"Are you kidding? No way, the universe has room for both of us, the kids need your message and mine and I think we can help each other. I think we can collaborate."* I told her how I admired her for developing such an awesome program and I really didn't want to do what she does. I just want to tell my own story. I can't tell her story.

What we also found out is that we both have skills in different areas and there's ways we can complement each other and work together, not compete with each other. Now that she doesn't see me as a threat or competitor she's going to have me speak at some of her events and I'm going to help her develop her book. Love it!

When you communicate with others and find ways to help someone else, they find ways to help you too. It's amazing, but it works.

I used to be jealous of other people's success, now I'm not because I'm creating my own success and the universe truly is full of abundance. The universe will never run out of stuff to give people, never! You just need to learn to ask for it. I know, the hardest thing to do is ask, but just do it. Who knows, you just may get the yes you're looking for and more.

I have learned that there is only one person I need to compete with and that's myself. As long as I am living up to my fullest potential and doing everything I can, then I am happy.

ACTION STEPS:

Write down ways that you can apply the Law of Reciprocation to your own life. What can you do to help others first, so that they want to help you too?

SECRET:

The more you help others, the more they want to help you.

Dear Kelly,

I think one of the most life changing perspectives we can hold is to learn to love ourselves unconditionally, always and forever, no matter what. We are all here for a reason and that unfolds during the course of our lifetime. Our journey can bring challenges, growing opportunities and some good life lessons. If we can focus on what we have done rather than what we have not, our self-esteem grows. If we look at where we are today from where we were yesterday or a year ago, rather than from where we interpret everyone else to be, our self-esteem grows.

If we look at what we can do instead of what we cannot or have not, our self-esteem grows. As we learn to celebrate our small wins each day, our self-esteem grows.

Loving ourselves unconditionally is much easier said than done. Sometimes we hang onto some life experiences or interactions with people that chipped away at parts of our confidence. Regardless of when it happened, if we are still carrying it we are allowing that to interfere with all we can be. We can consciously choose to find ways to release it and let it go, making room for bigger and brighter possibilities. How we focus on our life experiences either builds our confidence and appreciation of our self-worth or it takes away from it. We can gently love ourselves now as we blossom into who we want to grow to become. Love, compassion for our self and celebrating small wins are powerful foundations for growing self-esteem.

You are spreading a beautiful message Kelly.

Lisa Litwinski
Author, Facilitative Trainer, Speaker,
and Kaleidoscope Consultant ™
www.litpathlearning.com

ഇ ഇ ഇ

Dear Kelly,

The secret to my self-esteem is my strong belief that failure is not an option (and even if things don't go my way to learn from the lesson). When asked how I've achieved all that I have, I'm often mystified by the question. To me setting a goal and achieving it is as natural as breathing (although the outcome isn't always what I originally expect). Success is relative.

Let me explain. I don't really believe I am more successful than anyone else. I've reached a level of success that I've strived for because it's what I want and I believed I could achieve it. Believing in yourself is KEY to achieving any goal. What I want and what you want may be two completely different things and that's OK. As long as you believe in yourself and take action, you can accomplish your goals.

You should never let anyone but you determine your success, or failure for that matter. Plus, I believe success is ever evolving. What I want today may not be what I want tomorrow and I think that is part of the beauty of life (it's OK to change your mind). The most important thing is to enjoy life and do what you can to share your gifts with the world and most of all to believe in yourself.

Lisa Manyon
www.writeoncreative.com

ဟ ဟ ဟ

Dear Kelly,

I have always suffered from poor body image. And, I have felt powerless to do anything about it. I don't even try.

I am shocked when I see myself in pictures because they do not feel reflective of who I am.

A few years ago I attended a five-day retreat, where I had broken through emotional, mental and physical barriers, I knew then that I was forever affected and changed by the experience. I felt invincible. Everything seemed within the range of possibilities.

When I returned home, I met a few girlfriends for a birthday celebration and when I caught a glimpse of myself as I was passing by a full-length mirror, I stopped in my tracks. I looked gorgeous! My face was glowing. But what really amazed me was how sexy and svelte I looked. How womanly delicious.

It astonished me that as I changed the way I saw myself in my brain, it changed the way my brain saw my body. Not a single ounce of body fat was lost, but the weight of my heavy thoughts had lifted and I saw myself in an entirely different light.

It got me wondering whether anything we see is really real or if it is simply a reflection of the deeper relationship we are having with ourselves.

Farhana Dhalla
Author of Thank You for Leaving Me
www.FarhanaDhalla.com

CHAPTER 10

DON'T SWEAT THE LITTLE THINGS

"You DESERVE to feel great about you!"
~ Kelly Falardeau

I remember going to my Aunt Diane's house one day when I was in my early 20's and seeing a book entitled, *"It's Just a Little Thing."* And I believe it, most things we get upset about are tiny things that we make major issues out of.

Every time we spend energy making mountains out of mole hills, we get nowhere. All we do is add fuel to the fire. I've learned over the years to pick my battles - sometimes I'm right, sometimes I'm wrong.

Every time we get mad about something, it creates a negative energy around us and all we can do is get madder. Does it really matter that the guy in front of you cut you off? Seriously, what difference did that make in your life? So you had to slow down a bit, or steer out of his way. So what, you were probably going too fast anyways and needed someone to slow you down.

Why waste your energy getting angry? It's just not worth it and you might never see the person again anyways. So what, someone cut you off. It really isn't a big deal. I would rather spend my time being happy in my Happy Land than waste energy being mad at someone I don't know and never will know.

I'll never forget one time when I was wrong. It was a time when Max and I first got together and we didn't have a lot of money. We were invited to go to a baseball game with another couple. We bought the super extra large pop so we could share it and save money. We went to sit down and somehow Max knocked it over and the pop was all gone.

I got so mad I stood up and started yelling at him, because we didn't have any money to waste and how could he be so stupid to not see the pop right there beside him? I couldn't believe Max didn't dump me right then and there, I wasn't even thinking how I was making him feel. I didn't even think that other people could hear me yelling and I'm sure the people around us were thinking, wow, what a B*#^* she is to treat him like that, it was just a spilled pop. I couldn't believe how mad I got, it was just a pop!

I easily could have taken the cup and filled it with water, but no, I made a gigantic mountain out of that little mole hill. It totally wasn't right to treat Max that way. He didn't deserve that at all. It was just an accident. It was just a little thing, not worth getting upset about.

I'll never forget when I would talk to a certain friend on the phone. It never failed that when we would try to talk, her four-year-old son would want her attention too and she would start yelling at him. I couldn't believe how much she would yell at him and then come back on the phone and be sweet as ever on the phone with me.

It confused me, how could someone be so mad, mean and irate to a child she loved and then the next second be so completely sweet to me and it was like nothing even happened. Didn't she know I could hear her yelling at him? I was shocked and thought how sad it was that she could treat her son that she supposedly loved, in that way. Eventually I stopped being friends with her.

Let's talk about the toilet paper issue. You know what I'm talking about – does the toilet paper go over or under when it's on the toilet paper roller? Who cares! As long as it comes off the roll and I have something to use, then I'm happy. I just want a clean and happy butt and I don't care how it comes off the roll.

Is it really that big a deal? Max liked it over, so that's what we did. I honestly didn't care if I won that battle, it really didn't matter to me. It was a little thing, nothing worth wasting energy about. How about doing it like this; for one roll it's over and the next roll it's under? Or how about this; whoever replaces the roll, gets to choose? Seriously, does it really matter; is it really worth the fight?

Here's another crazy thing I did. When my kids were little and fascinated with nail polish, they really didn't want to paint my nails just one color. They wanted to use every color we had in the house and they all wanted a turn. It wasn't unusual for me to go to work with every toe nail and finger nail a different color. My friend Dawn would pick me up for work, look at my nails and say, *"Hmmm, nice nails Kel."* Yep, the kids did them again.

So what! Who cares? My kids had fun and I really didn't care if I was impressing anyone or not. Why would I deny my kids the happiness of painting their Mama's nails? There's no way I was going to say *"No, you can't do that because someone is going to think I'm ugly or crazy."* Again, your opinion of me isn't going to change my opinion of me.

I was building my kids' self-esteem by letting them show me how great they could paint my nails, even when they got it on my skin too. I certainly wasn't going to let them use nail polish on paper and their dad made it clear that boys don't wear nail polish. If it really bothered me, I could have cleaned it off, but I didn't.

Many times Max would come home from work and the kids had used water paints and painted my legs and arms. Well, the kids were covered too; they looked like those little kids from third world countries covered in war paint. I'm sure there were many times he was scared of what he was going to see when he came home from work.

I honestly thought it was a form of expression for the kids to experience while they were young, and even now if they wanted to.

The bottom line is, we had fun and all we had to do was go into the tub and have more fun with bubbles and getting clean. It was just a little thing, yeah so we got paint on the floor, oh well. It was a big mess, but it was worth the time cleaning up because we were laughing and had tons of fun.

I get so annoyed when someone has a little mole on their face and they use that as a reason to not feel beautiful. For some reason they think that people can't see their true beauty because they only see the mole. Really?

You really think you're ugly just because of that little mole? I've got more scars on my body than most people I know; how should I feel about myself if you feel ugly just with that little mole on your face?

If you feel ugly with that little mole, then I don't know what I should feel, is there any word that's worse than ugly?

People say I'm beautiful and I'm covered in scars, why wouldn't they think you're beautiful even with that little imperfection? Most people don't see that little thing that is bugging you that you're letting affect your whole self-esteem and control your thoughts.

People say to me, I'm going to be stared at because I have this scar on my face. SO WHAT! I have a gazillion scars, it doesn't stop me from feeling beautiful and why should it? I want to feel beautiful and I have every right to feel beautiful, I'm not going to let someone's stinking little opinion stop me. I don't need someone else's approval to feel beautiful and neither should you. Again, this reminds me of my quote – *your opinion of me isn't going to change my opinion of me.*

Even when people stare at me, all I do is IGNORE them! That's what I do. Yes, it gets annoying constantly having people stare at me, but it doesn't bother me anymore. I'm used to it. I just ignore them – so what if people stare, it isn't going to hurt me one bit if someone stares at me. I can't change what people are going to do and I can't change their thoughts, so who cares?

Some times when people stare at me, I just stare at them back. Some times I say to them, *"Hey, do I know you?"* Other times, when I was a kid, I would stick my tongue out at them or just turn around so they couldn't get a second or third look. People are going to stare whether you want them to or not and it doesn't matter if you have scars on your face or a mole or freckles, people are just naturally curious. Get over it, life is too short to be worried about other people's opinions of what they think you look like.

I honestly don't care if people don't think I am beautiful. It really doesn't matter. I've accepted that I only need to feel beautiful for me. I'm definitely not perfect and don't have the perfect body, but I'm beautiful anyways.

I don't need to have the perfect face or make-up or even the perfect hair or clothes to feel beautiful. I just need me.

ACTION STEPS:

Find something that bothers you and think of a way to make it fun or easier to handle.

SECRET:

You're perfect just the way you are.

Dear Kelly:

How do you 'really' see yourself? How do you value 'You'? How do you determine your own worth?

My answer: Self-esteem is a term used in psychology to reflect a person's overall evaluation or appraisal of his or her own worth. *(Wikipedia)*

Like many of you, I struggled with these issues for many years, from my childhood well into my adult life. Still do for very short times. There were times I wondered if I would ever amount to anything or accomplish anything of value. Then somewhere along the way things changed in how I valued myself and how I saw 'ME'.

Somewhere along the way I stopped worrying about what others thought and minimized how I compared to others or even to that 'ideal' picture of myself. I have worked diligently to close the gaps between my visualization of myself and where I really am at any given time.

I realize, I have room for improvement and strive to do so. I am learning to stop and savor the wins (even small ones) along the way. I am learning to graciously accept and evaluate the opinions and observations of others, whether positive or constructive. I am learning to allow myself to make a mistake or two along the way and to leverage those mistakes into greater accomplishments.

Here are a few quick ideas to help you create and maintain a healthy self-esteem:

1. Celebrate your achievements or wins, however small. Create a scrapbook (print or online) or a wall of fame where you display them. Then, revisit them from time to time. I did this with my hallway in my country place by providing a place for the plaques, awards, and designations earned. When I am assailed by self-doubt, I look at them and re-affirm I have accomplished some amazing things and I can do it again.

2.   *Create a warm fuzzy file where you store the nice things, the compliments, and the positive reinforcement people have given you. As a writer and speaker, I get notes and emails from people who appreciate what I have done. I put them in my warm fuzzy file and re-read them when needed.*

3.   *What do you do to feed your self-esteem? In addition to the above, what books (like this one) what tapes, CDs, or DVDs do you view? If you feed your self-esteem, you will grow stronger. Please remember to give yourself lots of love and positive self-talk to help build a healthier self-image.*

Self-esteem is a **build-it-yourself** *project. I am blessed to have a wife who loves me, a career that challenges me, friends and colleagues who enjoy me, and audiences and readers who appreciate what I say.* **As I see it…**

Bob 'Idea Man' Hooey
www.ideaman.net

ഔ ഔ ഔ

Dear Kelly,

The secret to my self-esteem is having a burning desire to change the world. After reading classics like Napoleon Hill's "Think and Grow Rich," Rollo May's "Man's Search For Himself, Jim Rohn's audio tapes, and countless others.

I realized that I feel fulfilled when I live an extraordinary life which really just involves being concerned about other people and helping them. In the words of Zig Ziglar:

"Help other people get what they want, and you can have everything you want." To summarize, the secret to my self-esteem is that everything has already been mapped out for us. We just have to have faith, persistence, work hard, and believe.

Keril Sawyerr
www.new-billionaires.com
www.createmarketingsystem.com

CHAPTER 11

PURPOSE + PASSION = POWER

"Forgot to put mascara on today, think anyone will notice? Nope, still got the inner beauty."
~ Kelly Falardeau

I love aha moments. When I get an aha moment, I get very excited. They're almost like an unexpected answer to a problem.

What is an 'aha' moment? An aha moment is one of those moments that you get when you're struggling to find an answer to something and then all of a sudden the answer pops into your head and you say *aha, that's it! That's the answer.*

People ask me, how do you get so many things done? How are you able to work at a full-time job, look after three kids, write a book, speak, build a business, do social media and everything else?

Because **I just do it**. When I get that aha moment, I run with it. I know that if I don't do *WHAT* inspires me, *WHEN* it inspires me, then I've lost the perfect moment and I've lost my energy for it. When I did the writing workshop, I participated in the class for nine-hours, drove home for three-hours, processed all the information in my head while I was driving and then spent three-hours writing when I got home.

That was the perfect moment for me to write. My head was bursting with information and stories I wanted to write about. If I would have waited until the next day or week to do it, I would have lost all the great energy and content. I had to write while it was there inside me and fresh in my mind. I didn't let any excuses get in my way. I wasn't even tired when I got home. I was energized and wasn't going to waste all that great energy by going to sleep. I was bursting at the seams and the only way to release it was to start writing at that very moment. ***You have to act on those aha moments WHEN you get them.***

Before I went to that writing workshop, I kind of knew what I wanted to write about, but nothing was defined or focused. I knew there was another book inside me, but I couldn't find it inside me at the time. After I took Kathleen Mailer's workshop, wow! I had my title, tagline, chapters and structure written by the end of the workshop. I now had the purpose and passion that I needed to write the new book. I was now focused and I didn't want to lose the momentum I had. **This is when purpose plus passion equals power.**

Once I defined the purpose of the book, the passion inside me ignited and that was all I could think about. All of a sudden, the content started flowing and I was full of all this incredible inspiration to write. And once I had the purpose and passion, an incredible power came over me.

I realized that people needed to read my story so that they too could learn my secrets to self-esteem. This book was no longer about me, it was about others and helping others to feel great and getting others to share their secrets too.

And since I have all three (purpose, passion and power), there's nothing that can stop me from achieving success with the book. The power is too strong inside me to quit. I learned of a quote by Douglas MacArthur, "Age wrinkles the skin. Quitting wrinkles the soul."

There was no way I could quit writing because I didn't want to wrinkle my soul. I had to act on the Purpose, Passion and Power that I had.

For example, here's what the typical person does. They take a seminar or workshop; they learn everything they can and then they go home and forget all about it and then they come up with millions of excuses as to why they didn't do anything with it. Not me – I take seminars and workshops because I want to learn how to do something and then I act on that passion. I do it. Simple as that, I act on the aha moment.

I could have easily gone home and made the excuse that I was too tired to write; after all, who wouldn't be tired after a nine-hour workshop and a three-hour drive home? Of course, absolutely, you're way too tired to write. But no way, I stayed up and wrote until midnight. Sleeping was not an option for me at that time, writing was the only option and I wasn't going to sleep until I had written down all my thoughts.

I completed my first 20-pages in three-hours. I love those aha moments. And now, everywhere I go, I carry my notepad with me because I don't ever want to lose a great thought.

I was looking for the missing piece of my puzzle and I found it at her workshop. For all you writers out there, you need Kathleen Mailer's workshop! With her workshop, you will be able to get your book completed and marketed. Check her out at the back of my book.

ACTION STEPS:

Think of a time when you had an aha moment. What did you do about it? Write down that aha moment and what you did about it. If you didn't do anything about it, what could you have done?

SECRET:

Act on the 'aha' moments when you get them; they are the bursts of energy that will help you succeed.

Dear Kelly,

I listened to my 17-year-old during an interview for her college and she sounded mature, wise and candid about her own strengths and weaknesses. When your child communicates in a way that speaks volumes of confidence and competence, that's when you know parenting, although THE toughest job on the planet, is well worth every second of time you invested. But her high self-esteem didn't come by way of chance; it came by my believing in her until she believed in herself.

As a teenager, I believed I was destined for failure in every way. Home life was abusively challenging and I was not blessed with brains or good looks. I did however, have a Sunday school teacher who said I was smart enough, pretty enough and loving enough, to be accepted by God. She told me often that nothing could stop me from doing great things in life - except me. Sometimes someone else needs to believe in us until we are able to believe in ourselves with faith, hope and love.

Self-esteem takes practice. My secret: Give yourself permission to create a routine of repeating how loved, cherished and important you are to God, to your family, to friends and those you will meet in the future. Believe in your own success so you can believe in the success of another when they can't do it for themselves.

Kellie Frazier
Matters of the Heart Specialist
www.ConnectingFHL.com

₨ ₨ ₨

Dear Kelly,

My secret to great self-esteem is to always have integrity in your relationships, finances and communications, and then there is no reason to doubt yourself or your decisions.

Kim Deep
www.thefamilywealthacademy.com

CHAPTER 12

FIND YOUR INSPIRATION

"If you want to meet someone that's TOTALLY AWESOME and REALLY SPECIAL....go look in the mirror..YOU (yes YOU) RULE!!!" ~ Bill Zucker

Something I noticed in the news is that there is tons of bad news. When you read the newspaper, 90% of it is bad and the rest is advertising. There may be one or two happy articles, but for the most part it's bad.

Even internet news is pretty much the same way, only I find there's more about which star is divorcing who or who's overcoming an addiction and in rehab. It's just generally bad and not very inspiring. Whenever I read the news, it doesn't inspire me, not even a little bit, so why would I pay attention to it? I don't even watch the news on television for the same reason.

It does nothing for my self-esteem, in fact, I think it's a waste of my time and energy to read or watch the news. Whenever I watch the news, I feel dull and unresponsive. What is the point in feeling that way?

It isn't unusual for me to not know about the latest hurricane or death or monster storm because I don't pay attention to the news. It's not that I don't care; it's just that if I take the weight of the world on my shoulders; there would be no reason to get out of bed in the morning. I'd be feeling so depressed that I wouldn't be able to inspire people because the world is so horrible.

At one time, I thought it was mandatory to watch the news. My grandpa did it every night and then my parents did it every day at supper time. I knew what time it was just by hearing the sound of the television and the opening song from the news.

But then I realized that I didn't have to watch the news just because my grandparents and parents did. I gave myself permission to stop hearing about all the bad stuff going on in the world.

I choose to listen to inspiring people and try to find the great stuff that is happening to keep me motivated and inspired.

I love to hear the news that my Champion Charmaine made the bestseller list and her and Toby her dog are inspiring the world. I like to hear about how my friend Troy Payne made the international bestseller list and how my small social media contribution may have helped him to succeed. I love to hear about my friends at FEAR.Less magazine (http://fearlessstories.com/) who are putting out this tremendous magazine about fearless people who are doing incredible things to change the world. Their magazine is full of inspiring stories.

I also love to read an online magazine that I write for called Special Living (http://www.specialiving.com). It's full of inspiring stories about people with disabilities and how they're making a great difference in this world. I also love reading my friend Tamara Plant's online magazine called the Mom Magazine (www.mommagazine.ca). I love how she's pushed the boundaries and been true and authentic to her quirky personality and writes about those topics that people are too scared to write about. Those are the news stories that I love to read about. I love to fill up my head with great inspiring stories, not negative uninspiring ones.

I also love reading news stories that my Facebook and Twitter friends post. If it's great, then I share it or retweet it so my friends can read it too. Like Scott

Stratten from Unmarketing says, "*Awesomeness spreads awesomeness, nobody spreads mediocre stuff, they want to spread about the awesome things people are doing.*" (http://www.unmarketing.com)

Do you really think that reading about how some guy murdered some gang member is going to inspire you to greatness? Not even a little bit, so why read about it and fill your head full of junk?

How about reading about Chad Hymas, a quadriplegic who won a gold medal in a wheelchair race? How does that make you feel? Makes me feel great that someone in a wheelchair doesn't let his disability stop him from accomplishing his dream. I love hearing about people's success stories. They help me to believe that I can be successful too. They help me to believe that the world is a great place to be.

For a long time, I didn't believe I could be successful. I believed that you had to be born with money in order to be rich. I also believed that success was defined by how much money a person had. Only the rich got richer is what I was taught. I could never be successful, just like I could never be beautiful. I think differently now.

When I stopped comparing myself to others and started creating my own life and my own passions, things started happening for me. When I stopped seeing things as obstacles and started seeing them as opportunities, things changed again. I believe that sometimes the universe puts up obstacles to help lead us onto a different path and usually a more '*correct*' one. The universe doesn't want us to fail and I believe that now.

For example, when I was seeking financing for my scrapbooking business to expand it, I had nothing but challenges thrown at me. It seemed no matter what I did, I couldn't make it happen. I even pitched my business on a reality television show and got right up to the finals, but one of the investors backed out at the very last minute. I was devastated.

Eventually, I decided to sell the business and sure enough a buyer came along and the deal went great and I pursued my passion for being a motivational speaker. And now that I'm pursuing that passion, everybody is helping me. They're giving me referrals and finding places for me to speak, they're sharing my book and my message; everything is coming together and falling into place. I am creating my own success, not someone else's.

I think the universe had this all lined up for me. The universe wants me to share my message and teach others how to have great self-esteem and I'm ecstatic about it, I'm loving it. I'm using my gift to serve others.

I believe that every time I got an opportunity to speak before I was a professional speaker that the universe was trying to point me in that direction. But I didn't know what was going on. I didn't know the universe was trying to point me in that direction until a couple years ago when my Champion Charmaine guided me.

It was almost like the universe said, *"Finally, she's following her passion and going in the direction we've been trying to lead her to. Watch her soar now."*

Another thing I believe is that the world is full of possibilities. Yes, full! Have you ever heard anyone say, there's nothing else the universe can give me? The world is endless and full of stuff to share. Whatever it is you want you can have, you just have to ask for it and take action.

But, beware, you can't always just wish for something and have it magically appear, you also have to take action to make it happen. For example, I want to buy a new vehicle, but I need to sell mine first. I haven't even put a for sale sign on it to let people know it's for sale.

How the heck is it going to sell if I don't even take the first step to try and sell it? If I don't put the wheels in motion to try and sell it, it won't sell. It's not magically going to sell itself. It needs me to take the first step, then the next step and then finally I'll have the vehicle I want.

Same thing goes for anything you want. You have to ask for what you want and then prove you really want it by taking the next step that is needed.

For example, I wanted to meet Ben Barry. He is responsible for convincing Dove to use real people as models in their beauty campaign. I wanted to meet him because I think we could do great work together. He could speak about body diversity and I could speak about inner beauty. He wasn't answering my emails and so I asked the universe for a way to meet him. Within days, I was presented with an incredible opportunity to meet Ben.

A model search competition was happening and Ben was a sponsor of the event. They were looking for an 'every day woman' not a typical model to win a one-year contract with his agency. Wow! Yep, the universe was listening and giving me what I wanted, an opportunity to meet Ben Barry. If I wouldn't have acted on that opportunity, do you think the universe would have given me another one?

I don't know, but I got the hint and acted on it. The universe can't send you an email or a text and say, *"Hey, I know you want to meet Ben so I'm going to create a modeling competition for you to enter so you can meet him."* No, he creates things and leaves you hints and signs and then you get to choose if you want to act on them or not.

When I saw the competition on Facebook, I knew that was the universe speaking to me and saying, *"Hey, you really want to meet Ben? Here's an opportunity."* I chose to take it. The total story of that journey is in my book 'No Risk No Rewards'.

As you start getting what you want in your life, your self-esteem starts building and it grows and grows because you're proving to yourself that yes you do deserve what you want in your life.

I'll never forget the day I told Max that I wanted to be a speaker. We were standing in the kitchen and I had just come home from a women's conference. I said to him, *"I'm going to be a speaker."* And he said to me, *"How are you going to do that?"* and I said, *"I don't know, but it's going to happen."* And sure enough, it did.

My first year, I had two speaking events and the next year 15. E-mails were flowing in, people wanted to hear my story and hear me speak and I trusted myself that I would become a speaker.

You see, success breeds more success. Happiness breeds more happiness. Anger breeds more anger. Discontent breeds more discontent. Ugly breeds more ugly. Beauty breeds more beauty. Whatever it is you're feeling, you'll breed more of it unless you shift your thinking to breed more of whatever it is that you really want.

For example, the more I thought I was ugly, the uglier I became. The more I thought I was unsuccessful, the more unsuccessful I became. When I stopped caring if others thought I was beautiful and gave myself permission to feel beautiful no matter what I looked like, then I felt beautiful. I shifted my thinking from I'm ugly to I'm beautiful and that's how I started feeling beautiful.

When I stopped being jealous of other's success and beauty, I started creating my own success and beauty. When I stopped focusing on all the bad stuff that was going on in my life and started seeing all the great stuff that was happening, I got more happiness.

I realized:

Beauty breeds beauty.

Success breeds success.

Happiness breeds happiness.

I said to myself, I wanted to be happy, beautiful and successful and now I have all three because I shifted my thinking from:

I'm ugly to: I'm beautiful.

I'm unsuccessful to: I'm successful.

I'm jealous to: I'm happy.

I'm discontent to: I'm content.

I'm ungrateful to: I'm grateful.

Nobody else can make me feel those things, only I can. I'm the one who has to think that way. Just like you're the only one who can create your own thoughts.

I'll never forget when I was being coached to walk the runway by a male coach. He was coaching 50 of us on how to walk like a runway model. He told me a million times how fabulous I was and every time he told me, I kept telling myself that he was full of crap. My brain didn't believe him and no matter how many times he told me I was fabulous, I couldn't shift my thinking.

I wasn't being authentic and that's why I couldn't believe him. As I was walking the runway it wasn't me being authentic, and as a result, I did a crappy job walking and I felt awkward and insecure. And I was so crappy that he made me do it twice! How come I couldn't feel fabulous, he told me a million times that I was?

Now, if he would have told me how fabulous I was when I was speaking, I would have believed him because I was being my authentic self and yes, I was then fabulous.

I know you're supposed to push your boundaries and try new things to make yourself grow. I did that when I walked the runway and as a result I realized that I wasn't a model, I was a speaker.

Even though I felt so awkward, I am glad that I did it. That experience helped me to realize where my true story was. My story is about my inner beauty, self-esteem and taking risks. And like my mother always said, "*Outer beauty is only skin deep, ugly is right to the bone.*"

Walking the runway also taught me that it takes a lot of courage and skill to be a runway model; I'd rather speak and show those skills instead. I got great satisfaction when I did my speeches, but I didn't feel the same way when I was walking the runway.

ACTION STEPS:

Write down what inspires you. In your ideal life, what are you doing that will fulfill you and make you happy? What are you jealous of and how can you change it so you can be successful. What can you do to create success in your life? Write down what makes you authentic.

SECRET:

Be your authentic you and you will be successful.

Dear Kelly,

Healthy self-esteem is about being comfortable in your own skin. It is ultimately about loving who you are and knowing you are worthy of all the great things life has to offer.

No one else possesses your skills and abilities and serves others in your way. God does not make mistakes so why rob the world of what they are waiting for!

There are two particular events in my life which occurred only months apart in which people's opinions defined my reality for a short time. In the final months of my senior year in high school, I told a boy that I was not interested in pursuing a relationship with him. He wrote a lengthy letter just before I left for university about how I better use my brains for something because I did not have much of a body.

I couldn't believe someone could say such terrible things. I read it over and over in disbelief until one day my friend Brian read it and ripped it up right in front of me and said, "You do not need to read this anymore. You are so much more." One person's opinion did not matter. What mattered is what I thought.

As a child I loved watching Miss Canada and the other beauty pageants, like you, Kelly, I was in a beauty pageant. The experience was phenomenal. One night, a few of the girls and I went out together and one of them said, "Oh, you must have lost a few pounds to wear that." I was in complete disbelief as I replayed her comment in my head that evening. I was 125-pounds at the time – 7-pounds heavier than any of the other girls. I was healthy, vibrant and one of the top ten finalists. I must have had something that the judges liked. I was real and I loved people.

Over the years, I have reflected on these situations, separating fact from fiction and realized that I have so many gifts to offer and share. One of the greatest lessons I must share with you is – you are so much more than your body or outside appearance. Your body is an amazing machine which you should value and take care of. Every scar, stretch mark, or mole is about who you are; they are part of your story.

My body has endured delivering babies, sprinting through a triathlon, and hugging people who needed to feel loved and appreciated. I am so much more and so are you. I know now, you can have both beauty and brains so watch out world, here I come. As in the words of Lady Gaga, I was "born this way!"

Kelly, you have beauty and brains and you are constantly evolving into a new and improved you each day. People will always have their opinions but it is just that – one person's opinion. Beauty does not come from a bottle; it comes from within.

Debra Kasowski
www.themillionairewoman.com

ഇ ഇ ഇ

Dear Kelly,

The secret to my self-esteem is never forgetting I'm a watch, and God is the watchmaker. If I can accept that I am a product of an elegant universe, then I too must be elegant. The acorn can only come from a mighty oak. I never forget that I am also a product of love. Thus, I am love. As long as I remember who I am and never put my value in the hands of others, I can be at peace with my role in the universe. To the degree that we love, we are loved. Everything is a reflection of me and I of it. Separation is an illusion. We are one; we are love. Love does not have to question the value of its worth because it lives in the world of gratitude.

Fred Cuellar
www.diamondcuttersintl.com

ഇ ഇ ഇ

Dear Kelly,

Thank you for the opportunity to share my thoughts on what may contribute to my sustainable self-esteem. While many factors come to mind, the secret to my self-esteem is rooted in my belief that:

- *life is the most precious gift any of us will ever receive; and*
- *the vast majority of people are fundamentally good.*

Since life is precious, I am grateful and joyful to be alive. Since people are fundamentally good, most will value me as a human being, and I can look past the rare times that some of them don't appear to do so.

In other words, my self-esteem is not based on my status, accomplishments, or what others say or do. It is hard-wired in me as a human being who is very grateful for this wonderfully thrilling ride we call "life."

Dune Nguyen, MBA, CMC, PMP, ISP
Management Consultant, Educator & Entertainer
www.dunenguyen.com

CHAPTER 13

SET YOURSELF UP FOR SUCCESS, NOT FAILURE

"When you demand to be perfect, you set yourself up for failure; when you strive to be near-perfect, you succeed every time." ~ Kelly Falardeau

"Just because you aren't perfect, it doesn't mean you aren't beautiful." ~ Kelly Falardeau

I have a cousin who I have always thought was very beautiful. She has the most gorgeous eyes and when I look at her I see instant beauty, but she doesn't see herself that way at all. She sees herself as not being *'perfect'* and since she isn't perfect, she isn't beautiful.

She hates her looks and as a result hates herself. She thinks she's fat and ugly, not near-perfect and beautiful. She sees her fat, moles and prickly, flabby skin on her arms, but doesn't see her great eyes and fabulous smile and great sense of humor. I think it's so sad that she constantly picks on herself and can't find her true beauty and won't give herself permission to feel beautiful because she isn't perfect.

One day we were at my sister's baby shower and my cousin was there and she was showing me a picture of her six-year-old son. I said, *"Wow, doesn't he ever look great, he's sure a handsome little guy."* Her comment was, *"Hmmm, I don't think so, could be better."* I was shocked!

I couldn't believe that she didn't think her six-year-old son didn't look perfect. I didn't think he could look any more perfect at all. I was also sad because I thought, how sad is that that she believes her son doesn't have the perfect looks.

Seriously, there was nothing wrong with that picture. I should have asked her what would he have to do for her to think his picture was perfect?

I don't believe that you have to have the perfect body in order to feel beautiful.

I am so far from being perfect and having the perfect body that I know being perfect is impossible, unachievable and highly over-rated; but, *I think being near-perfect is perfect enough for me.*

Have you ever heard a perfectionist say that something is perfect? Seriously? That's the problem with being a perfectionist - nothing is ever perfect enough. People put so much pressure on themselves to be perfect that they set themselves up for failure before they even start.

Every time I tried to achieve perfectionism I failed, nothing was ever good enough, but every time I tried to achieve near-perfect, I succeeded, every time! And my brain feels so great that I'm able to accept that I don't have to be perfect, I just need to be near-perfect. Even my book '*No Risk No Rewards*' isn't perfect. I didn't try to achieve perfectionism because I knew it was impossible for me, but I wanted to feel like I succeeded and so I strived for **near-perfect** and guess what? I succeeded!

Yes, you will find mistakes in my book and I know where they are, it's definitely not perfect. I had at least five people proofread my book and including myself, I'm sure I read it at least 1000 times.

That's why I had other friends proof it and yet, I still found more mistakes after it was published. But, you know what? My book is near-perfect and that's perfect enough for me. I succeeded; I accomplished something I didn't think I could do and I get to share my story with people who need to be helped. So, yes I am a success and proud of myself for creating my book, especially because the year before, I didn't think I had enough content to even write a book.

So let me tell you how far away from being perfect my body is. I am so imperfect, that it would take a million dollars and a million surgeries to make me physically perfect and I still wouldn't be perfect! I feel so sad for people who think their body has to be perfect so someone else can think they're beautiful.

For some reason, me with the most imperfect body gets told that I'm beautiful, fabulous, gorgeous, sexy, hot and yet I have a crooked arm, crooked fingers, a bald spot, scars all over my face, chest, back, arms and legs, big lips, a deformed ear, a missing nipple and my breasts are too low. And yet somehow I feel **greater than great.** You know why? Because I'm near-perfect and I'm as good as I'm going to get and I love the things I love about me.

I love my big beautiful green eyes, I love my cute little nose, I love my little deformed ear (and could never live without it, even though at one time I wanted to get it fixed) and I love that I can make people laugh and I love my kids and how, no matter what I look like, I'm perfect enough for them.

My kids have never told me they wished I looked different. In fact, none of my family or friends have said, *I wish you didn't have scars so I could love you more.* So yes, I'm perfect just the way I am and that's one of the reasons I just love Pink's song Fn Perfect. My kids know me as a beautiful mom just the way she is and I wouldn't have it any other way.

I'll never forget when I met one of my dearest burn survivor friends, Lynda Fraser. She had just gotten burnt and I went to visit her in the burn unit at the hospital. I was a little shocked when I met her because she didn't have a nose; she just had two holes in the middle of her face where her nose would have been if it hadn't have been burned off. I had never seen a face without a nose before!

She got burnt as an adult (I think she was about 35-years-old) and her son was playing with matches and she rescued him and as a result ended up with very severe burns to her face, chest, arms and legs and her son only had minor burns on his hands.

I always admired Lynda because no matter what, she perservered and realized that she too deserved to feel beautiful even with her scars. She saw herself go from a beautiful perfect woman to a beautiful scarred woman and accepted her new body as near-perfect.

I love this comment Lynda made on my Facebook wall about being different:

> *"My mom always says if she won the lotto she would find the best surgeon in the world and have him 'fix' my face....she doesn't get it, I like my face just the way it is....and the advantage to my burn scars is, it is so tight I won't get any wrinkles so it will basically stay this way for the rest of my life!!! Can so-called 'normal' people say they will always have the same face, lol."*

I hope you will find a way to be **near-perfect** and not be so hard on yourself. Being perfect really is impossible, unachievable, highly overrated and a whole lot of pressure. Seriously, do you really think your friends aren't going to love you because you have a few wrinkles on your forehead? You really think you need that Botox to make you feel better and look more beautiful?

ACTION STEPS:

Make a list of things that you strive for complete perfection about. Write down the pressure you feel by not achieving perfection. What do you need to do so you can be near-perfect and allow yourself to feel successful.

SECRET:

Near-perfect is possible, achievable and perfect enough for me.

Dear Kelly,

Self-esteem isn't something you are born with; it is grown and nurtured throughout life. It can also be snapped like a twig in lightning speed. I know this to be true. Being teased severely throughout elementary school put my self-esteem in the toilet.

With help and support from family and the few friends I did have in elementary school, I was able keep believing in myself and keep my light shining. I know some may find positive self-talk hokey; however, I believe that it is what also got me through. I kept telling myself that I was beautiful, that I was pretty, that I was smart and still am.

I continue to do the positive self-talk even to this day, it's just a little reminder to keep my inner light shining. I also now don't worry as much about what others think of me, I know in my heart that I am awesome.

Hugs,
Aime Hutton
www.awakeninggoddess.com

My dearest Kelly,

I applaud and fully support your endeavours to spread the message that 'each and every one of us is truly worth it'!

It is also indeed an honour and privilege to share some insights into my recipe for esteem. To fully appreciate and comprehend the desired end product of my recipe, we need to keep in clear focus an operational definition of self-esteem: What our unconscious believes to be true about how worthy, lovable, valuable, and capable we are. Our esteem starts with and rests with ourselves. We must realize that we humans can never attain perfection as that exists only in a Divine power to whomever we may ascribe that position.

Sam Keen so aptly states:
"We come to love by not finding a perfect person, but by learning to see an imperfect person perfectly." Our quest to see 'the imperfect person we are' perfectly speaks loudly to both our perspective and perception of ourselves. An attitude of positivity accompanied by unconditional love for ourselves must be at the root of our personal perspective and perception.

Sprinkle in a generous modicum of positive self-talk and an environment of similarly minded folks for support with a continual dash of success-promoting situations and stir in spontaneous celebrations of each and every success no matter the magnitude of your success. As our personal positivity and unconditional love soar, our esteem blossoms and we become that 'imperfect person seen perfectly' both by ourselves and the world. Cultivating one's personal esteem is one of the greatest gifts one can regularly give oneself!

Respectfully submitted,
Murray Douglas
A life-long professional educator

CHAPTER 14

FIND YOUR GIFTS YOU CAN SHARE

"Why change yourself to look like someone else when there is only one authentic, original and unique you."
~ Ben Barry

I had the great honour and pleasure of speaking at the World Burn Congress in Texas, and not just once but twice. I was asked to be a co-presenter about Blogging and Writing for Fun and Soul plus a panel member on the Sexuality and Intimacy session.

On the first day I was there, I went to the morning session and listened to Dan Caro speak. Dan was a fantastic speaker. He also got burnt when he was two-years-old (like I did) and as a result he lost all his fingers on both hands. When a burn survivor has no fingers, they call their hands 'paws.'

Dan wanted to be a drummer but only had paws, no fingers, so how was he going to hold his drumsticks? The incredible thing is that he didn't let his paws stop him from becoming a drummer and he found a way to hold drumsticks. Not only did he do that, but he also became one of the top 500 drummers in the United States. Wow, how incredible, I love his story.

As I was hearing him speak, I was mesmerized. I thought wow, how incredible that he can speak like this with no notes and make it look so natural and easy plus he's so inspiring. After he spoke there was a break and so I went outside to text my best friend about Dan and tell him how amazing he was. I texted, *"How am I going to do what he does and what do I have to offer these burn survivors?"* This conference had 850 of the most severely burned burn survivors. And a lot of them had just got burnt.

Some of them had missing arms and legs and faces and were severely disfigured; others weren't so badly burned. Some were burned as children, others adults.

I didn't feel like I had anything to offer the burn survivors and their families. I started crying and walking and I kept texting my friend. He told me that I needed to speak, that these people needed to hear from me. They needed to hear my story and that I had a purpose and that my dad, God and himself were all there with me in spirit. I kept crying and walking. I couldn't see ahead, I just followed where the sidewalk took me. I kept telling my friend that I didn't know what I could offer them and he kept telling me that I had to speak no matter what.

But then I stopped walking when I came to the end of the sidewalk and looked up and there was the street sign that said it all. The street sign said "Hope Blvd." Oh my goodness, there was my gift and my sign from the universe. I could give them "**Hope.**"

I texted my friend and said, *"You'll never guess what I just saw, a street sign that says Hope Blvd, I guess that's what I can do, I can give them hope."* And he said, *"Yes, give them hope and now go rock it."* I turned around and went back to the conference. The next day I went back and took a picture of the street sign so that I could blog about it.

When I decided I wanted to be a speaker, I took a keynote coaching program from Cheryl Cran. This workshop taught me a lot of great things, but the biggest thing it taught me was that it's not about me, it's about '**them.**'

That's when I realized that my talent for speaking was a gift. I don't speak because I want to be the center of attention on the stage, I speak because I want to share my stories with others and help others to become an amazing person full of great self-esteem and inner beauty.

I want you to realize that dreams are meant to be found, not tucked away in dreamland. I want you to give yourself permission to feel great about yourself. I also want you to feel like you deserve to have a fantastic life, no matter how many scars, moles or how overweight you are. I want you to know that you shouldn't let other people's opinions stop you from feeling great about yourself. I want to share my gift with others because if a burn survivor with a body full of scars can feel great, then so can you. Those are my gifts for you.

I'll never forget one day when I met a man named John Oldham. I was in Starbucks, playing with my iPad and he was sitting at the table next to me. He asked me what I thought of my iPad and I gave my honest opinion and we started having a great conversation. It turned out that he was a retired school principal from my town that I grew up in. I told him that I was an author and speaker speaking about inner beauty and self-esteem and he was telling me about his NuSkin business and how fantastic he was doing with it. I was thoroughly impressed with his success and it turned out that a few of my friends were a part of his team.

John asked to know more about my book and so I gave him one to look at. He was embarrassed that he didn't have $20 cash on hand to buy it so he asked if I would want to trade him for the book he had. He found his book 'Aspire' to be a tremendous inspiration for him and helped him to grow personally.

I said that I would love to trade books with him, but the other issue was that he didn't have another one with him and that he would have to get back in touch with me so that he could give me a copy of his book. I said '*no problem*', and we exchanged business cards. For some reason, I just had a great feeling about John.

John also proceeded to tell me about his book '*Aspire*' some more and how at the back of the book is the "Book of Greats" and there is 10 topics and whenever you find someone who you believe fits one of those 10 topics, you are to ask them to sign your "Book of Greats." He told me that it would be a great gift to him if I would sign the "inspire" section of his Book of Greats. I could tell that he was emotional about it as his hands were shaking and his voice slightly trembling and I could just feel his passion. As I signed it, I felt deeply honoured that he asked me to sign it for him.

The story doesn't end there, a couple days later, I was rushing to a speaking event and I had runs in my nylons and I had to run to the store to get more. Normally a run doesn't bother me, but I had four of them in one pair of nylons! I was buying my nylons and there was John. We bumped into each other and I said, "*Wow, we just met and now we see each other twice in one week, how funny.*" The very next day John called and made arrangements to get me his book, '*Aspire*.'

A few weeks later I called John about something and he said to me, "*Kelly, I feel really bad; I really should have paid you for your book. What an awesome book, I really should have paid you money for it, I'm not happy about this.*" And I said to him, "*No John, I am happy with the deal and totally ok, we made a trade, book for book and I feel that someday you will repay me with something far greater than money. Please, accept my gift and don't worry about paying me money, I won't accept it.*"

I shared my gift with him and I know that someday he wants me to speak for him and share my message with his friends. That is what I love about John and NuSkin, it's all about personal development and if you help others to feel great, then you will feel great too.

When you find ways to share your gift, more greatness will come to you. When all you do is find the crappy things in people and find ways to gossip about them, it just brings you down too. John found a way to give me a gift (even though he said it was a gift to him) by asking me to sign his Book of Greats; I was honoured and humbled. I never thought I could be considered good enough to be in someone's Book of Greats, but he thought I was and that's all that mattered. I gave him the gift of my book and the inspiration that he found in it. Together we both gave each other gifts and that was a great feeling.

Another example of a gift is my best friend's daughter Kat. She has a phenomenal gift of drawing. She has this amazing talent and she's only 14-years-old. What drives me crazy is that she doesn't think she's good enough; although, everyone who has seen her artwork says she's fantastic. She is actually very shy about her work.

I asked her to do a cartoon drawing of a girl for my Self-Esteem ROCKS for Youth program. I sent her a picture of a style I was looking for plus I told her I wanted her to have dirty blond/brown hair, freckles and brown eyes. Kat said to me, "*Hey, that describes me.*" So she drew this fantastic drawing and I put it on Facebook and a whole bunch of my friends were commenting on how great it was.

Kat got on my Facebook wall and saw that everyone was commenting on how great she was and thanked everyone for the compliments. I totally enjoyed sharing Kat's gift with my friends because not only did we all believe that she did great, it also gave Kat recognition that others did too. It helped her to realize that she truly has a gift.

I wanted to help Kat realize that her gift and passion is her drawing and when you find your passion, you need to follow it. You see, when she started drawing for me and I was encouraging her, she felt great and empowered. We worked together to create these cool drawings that everyone loves.

I wanted to share Kat's gift one more way; somehow I wanted to include her drawings in my book and so that is why I had her draw my twins too and her drawings are in the front as a dedication to my kids.

Kat: Please don't ever give up on your passion, you are a fabulous artist and that incredible feeling you get when you draw something is your passion and great things happen when you follow your passion.

Something that Janet Attwood from 'The Passion Test' taught me was that when you are making a decision between two things, you need to choose in favour of your passion because when you do, it takes you in the direction of your passion.

ACTION STEPS:

Write down what your gifts are. What gives you that incredibly great feeling? What is it that you love to do and don't want to stop doing? Find ways to share your gifts.

SECRET:

Find your gifts and share them.

Dear Kelly,

For me, great self-esteem is a kind of calm confidence in knowing I've done the right thing and that I've done it well. But even more so it comes from doing something for others. Especially passing on information that may help them in the current situation they are in at this point in life.

I can exercise, meditate, work or educate myself all I want, but the gratification of that is shallow compared to what it feels like to walk out the door to the world filled up with that sense that you just etched in a positive difference in a person's life.

To see the look in their eyes, to hear the "Ah-ha!" in their voice and to know that they can now move ahead in their life is so fulfilling that it causes me to keep on dealing with life in a very positive manner.

The esteem that it builds is priceless. There is a saying from Shantideva: "All the suffering in the world comes from self-cherishing. All the happiness in the world comes from cherishing others."

Of course we still have to care for ourselves and have self-love otherwise we can't even help others, yet even when we are not in our 'happy place' at certain times - once we get involved with assisting someone else, we forget all of our problems!

Rick Titan
www.razorricktitan.com

ജ ജ ജ

Dear Kelly,

The secret to my self-esteem is that I write the script of my life. I write the "classified ads," for the people I attract. One day I was hanging out with my friends and was acting out like I was at a Wild West saloon and saying things like, "I am powerful, and I want to show you some of my experiences and my discoveries. Girls, I am bulletproof and you can be bulletproof too!"

I had said this like a robot, over and over and over, to my friends. Without even realizing it, I had planted seeds in their minds about how I function. From there it was a short jump to an 'aha' moment—"That's it!" my friends exclaimed, "God is her Sugar Daddy, and he rides the range looking for outlaws!"

A lot of people judged me solely by my looks, or my life circumstance, and the fairy tale romance, between me and God himself as my 'Sugar Daddy,' a Cinderella-type picture.

A Barbie doll life, fit perfectly on my little girl size-zero frame. I may be delicate, and I might be easy on the eyes and might not be taken seriously at first, but this is one woman who always kept her eye on her goal to rise above humble beginnings, but always seemed to have a "spiritual coach," an action hero universe. Someone who was looking out for her, building her up, and making sure her 'supply valve' was wide open to receive! Even through devastating twists of fate and scores who lined up to oppose her at every step, it was obvious to us all, that there was some sort of inexplicable 'divine intervention,' going on; she would call it her supernatural wild west 'Sugar Daddy,' and he was looking out for this girl!

Girlfriends saw magic happening in the blonde's life and they wanted to know how to get theirs! Come on LuAn cough it UP, how do we get one of those, how do we make God our 'wild west' Sugar Daddy too, please tell us?"

I'd already come far when my husband's family meat packing business fell into my lap, and no one was going to stop me from going into the slaughterhouse and kicking some ass, so I could take it from the brink of bankruptcy to a $450 million company.

And that's the whole point; my life is a testament that someone can, take off and reach imagined heights, take a fresh perspective and look at themselves and the world differently. We can show that every life has meaning, but beware; it is your life, your movie, your classified ad.

Don't let someone else label you or put you in a box; let that wild and wonderful person who is inside of you, (and your own brand of universal 'Sugar Daddy') come out to play. You can be all that you envision. Don't drift away in a prevailing wind; don't be torn by every criticism. Be a Wild West hero, learn to dodge bullets, learn to LOVE, and be grateful for it all.

My rollercoaster life has, indeed, been lived in the headlines; sharing it with a broader public through lectures, TV appearances, my radio program and in my books, together with other authors who share stories as well, on this mission just like me is how I give back and plant seeds every day. It is both my mission and my passion, and I do it by being totally honest and open about my life and what I have learned and what I still learn every day.

LuAn Mitchell
www.theLuAnMitchell.com

CHAPTER 15

CELEBRATE YOUR LITTLE SUCCESSES

*"It is not enough to recognize the fire,
YOU MUST dance with it."* ~ Fred Cuellar

People wonder how come I have so much great news and other exciting stuff all the time. I've trained myself to celebrate my small successes and each of those little successes eventually leads to bigger successes.

Every little success I have counts, just like every success you have counts too! Every time something good happens in my life, I tell myself about it and celebrate it by announcing it on Facebook and Twitter. Every time when I look in the mirror and say to myself, *"Wow, you look hot today,"* or every time I announce on Facebook that I've had a little success, it builds my self-esteem. My self-esteem gets bigger and bigger and my brain realizes that yes, I am a success and yes I deserve even more success. I am training myself how to feel great about me. In this case, it's all the little stuff that will build me up to feel great.

You see, people want to know about the success we're having, people want to be able to promote us and tell the world about how great we're doing. People want to know successful people. They want to see average ordinary people succeed. When people like you and I become successful, it helps them to believe that they can do it too. Success isn't just for the Oprah Winfreys of the world, it's for everyone.

If you keep beating yourself up and focusing on all the bad stuff you have going on in your life then you will never feel great about yourself. That's why I celebrate all the great stuff I have in my life.

For me, it's also a way that I show that I'm grateful for everything I have in my life. I am always thanking people for helping me succeed or for writing about me or for anything that they do for me.

I'll never forget one day I was feeling pretty crappy. There was a situation that happened and it was really bothering me. I texted my best friend and told him what was going on and he texted me a couple pictures of flowers from his garden. Then I got two emails from customers who wanted to book me and then Max texted me about something and we were laughing about it and then something else great happened.

So then, I decided it was time to count my blessings and all the great things that happened that day. By noon, I had 23 things to be thankful for and only one thing that made me miserable. And by doing that little exercise, I realized that I had way more stuff to be grateful for than upset about and I happened to forget what I was mad about. All the blessings I had far outweighed what I was mad about.

I realized that you have to have an "*attitude of gratitude*" in order to succeed in life.

For example, I wrote an article about Chad Hymas for a magazine called Special Living. This magazine celebrates all the great stuff that people with disabilities are doing and he's one of them. Not only did Special Living like the article I wrote, but they used it as a cover story and was I ever ecstatic. They didn't tell me that they were going to use it as the cover story. Wow!

I was having a crappy day and it didn't seem to matter what I did, I couldn't shift my thinking and create positive energy around myself. I was being a brat and calling myself names and even saying things to hurt my best friend and crying my eyes out and just being nasty to myself. But then I got the news from Betty that the latest 'Special Living' issue was released and my story was on the cover.

I read the article and was I ever excited that they used it for the cover, so of course I changed my status on Facebook to say, *wow, I'm so excited, was having a crappy day, but just found out my article about Chad Hymas made the cover.* Instantly my self-esteem felt great because I celebrated my little success and I shifted my thinking and realized that I did have something to be grateful for.

And then, it gets better, Chad posted on my Facebook wall a thank you for writing about him and how he loved the article. And then he went on his Facebook wall and posted how honoured and humbled he was that I wrote this awesome article about him and how it made the cover of this amazing magazine.

Do you see what's happening? My little success that I celebrated is turning into an even bigger success. I wrote about Chad, my article got published as a cover story (awesome, Kelly girl), my friends comment on how awesome the article is, Chad then notices me, thanks me then talks about me and he has over 5000 friends (awesome, awesome Kelly girl), Chad's mom personally emails me thanking me, what's next?

Maybe I'll get to meet him in person, or maybe he'll write a little something for my book or maybe he'll help me promote my new book or maybe he'll invite me to speak at an event with him. Not sure what's going to happen next, but my self-esteem is feeling great because I celebrated that little success of announcing on Facebook about my cover story.

I helped Chad and not only am I feeling great but so is he. He said how honoured and humbled he was that I wrote such a terrific article about him. And you know what? I only met Chad on the internet, he doesn't even know me and I haven't even heard him speak other than on his website.

His speaking video had me inspired in less than 10-minutes. Want to know another thing? Technically, I could consider Chad a competitor, we're both inspirational speakers. How many people do you know help their competitors? I don't consider Chad a competitor; the universe is full of abundance and I know that when you help someone achieve success you will achieve success too. I also know that Chad and I both share different messages and the world needs to hear both.

So not only did I celebrate my little success which was turning into a much bigger success, but I also practiced the Law of Reciprocation. *The Law of Reciprocation says that you need to first help others achieve what you want to achieve.* So in my case, I write about people who inspire me and in return people write about me because I inspire them too.

Another thing I do is help others become a success, because I want to be a success too. I still remember Darren Jacklin telling me about that law a few years ago. I didn't really understand it until I started seeing it work for me. I realized that the more I started giving to others, the more I started getting back. You help others first and you will receive back.

ACTION STEPS:

Write down what you want to achieve in your life. Write down a list of people you want to help so that they can turn around and help you too. Write down what you are grateful for.

SECRET:

The more you help others, the more they want to help you back.

Dear Kelly,

My "secret" to great self-esteem is knowing that no one's opinion or thoughts about me contribute to who I am. I am perfect and beautiful, I am connected to everyone and everything, I am who you are and I am in competition with no one. Knowing this brings peace to my heart, love in my life and light all around me. Peace, Love and Light will give anyone an amazing self-esteem. Whenever I begin to forget or doubt these things, I repeat them back to myself as affirmations.

Troy Payne
www.wellnessrealization.net

೫ ೫ ೫

Dear Kelly,

I have two secrets; one is a quote I came up with and a quote by Tim Johnson:

"At ALL cost, protect your SELF confidence." by Tim Johnson

And

"BE curious about everything, BE open to anything, only to BEcome a master of a few things!" by John Su

John Su
www.ImperialInvestmentRealty.com
www.InvestorSage.Wordpress.com

೫ ೫ ೫

Dear Kelly,

My secret to great self-esteem is: worry more about how you see yourself and less about the way other people see you.

Amber Wladyka

CHAPTER 16

DE-CLUTTER YOUR HEAD

"Dreams are meant to be found, not tucked away in Dreamland" ~ Kelly Falardeau

Stop getting so mad about everything;

Stop complaining;

Stop grumpy gossiping;

Stop worrying;

Fill up your head with the great stuff instead of all that clutter.

Did you know that 90% of what you worry about never happens? So why are you spending so much time worrying about something that will more than likely not happen? You have to learn how to trust yourself and not worry so much about stuff. All worrying does is clutter up your head with useless junk and takes up precious space in your head and doesn't allow room for great stuff that will inspire you to greatness.

Gossip is another pile of junk you don't need in your head. The more you grumpy gossip about someone, the more you knock them and yourself. I know some times when I grumpy gossip about someone, I start to feel guilty because I never know if they're going to find out what I said and then they're going to get mad at me for gossiping about them. Plus I also don't feel it's right to talk about someone behind their back. And inevitably there will be some hard feelings; and then I will have to spend time smoothing things over. I also noticed that when I gossiped, it didn't make me feel good. So why do it?

If you want to gossip, spread good gossip about your friends and family. There's nothing like good gossip! There's been times when I've heard from friends that they were at a women's convention and ran into someone else who knew me and they started talking about how great I was, not how crappy I was, and how they loved my message and the work I'm doing. Good gossip helps to spread awesomeness plus builds great self-esteem.

Think about how great you feel when you spread good gossip. Think about all the positive energy that surrounds you and your friends you were talking with. Did you notice your energy and motivation going up?

Remember the Law of Reciprocation – if you want good gossip spread about you then you have to spread good gossip about someone else *first*.

Every time you get mad about something, you bring negative energy to yourself and create more bad vibes. Find ways to be happy, not mad. The happier you are, the greater self-esteem you'll have.

I have to admit, that there is definitely something that men do better than women and that is they can have an argument with their best buddy and then five minutes later go have a beer and be back to best friends again. Women really do have to learn how men do that.

Seriously, when women have an argument with their girlfriends, they fight and then harbor it for months and months and a lot of times lose their friendship over it. Totally sad that women hold grudges as long as they do.

I'll never forget two incidences I had with one of my best girlfriends Janeen. We used to work at the same place together and she had just gotten a promotion and didn't have as much time for me as she did in the past. We couldn't go for cherry Cokes any more, which was our favorite thing to do at lunch time. So one time I said to her, *"Hey, now that you're a big wig, you don't have time for me any more."*

Well, Janeen did the best thing she could have, she stopped me right there and said immediately, *"You just hurt my feelings"* and instantly I apologized. I was just joking; I wasn't trying to hurt her feelings. A lot of women would get really upset and go tell all their friends and make a huge mountain out of a little mole hole and then it would turn into a major disaster, but not Janeen, she told me right away that I hurt her feelings and we dealt with it right then and there and were back to being best friends.

Another time, she hurt my feelings, but I did the normal thing to her. I went about being like a normal woman and harbored the feelings and decided to ignore and avoid her. She called me many times and I completely avoided her calls. Until one time she left a message and said, *"Kel, please I need you and I don't want our friendship ruined, please tell me what is wrong so we can deal with it."* And so, I talked to her and told her my point of view and she told me her point of view and then things were fine, we were back to being the best of friends.

The bottom line is, I would be devastated without her friendship. She is one of my Champions and without her, I'd be lost and so whenever we have a problem with each other we always talk about it instead of ignoring the situation.

When I was a kid, I used to watch horror movies because that was what all the other kids did. I used to get so freaked out, I couldn't sleep for days and I believed that those things really did happen to people. I would have dreams of horrible images and was petrified that those things were going to happen to me too.

It took me a long time to realize that I didn't have to watch something that was just going to scare the pants off me and for no good reason.

Garbage in garbage out, goodness in goodness out.

ACTION STEPS:

Evaluate what you are doing in your life to clutter your head. Find ways to eliminate the clutter so you can fill yourself up with great stuff.

What kind of energy do you feel when you're doing grumpy gossip? What kind of negative energy are you creating around yourself? Write down situations where you grumpy gossiped and situations where you spread good gossip. Write down times you good gossiped about someone and record how you felt when you did that.

SECRET:

Fill your head with great stuff that makes you feel great about yourself.

Dear Kelly,

My secret to great self-esteem is....always know what you are worth.

I may be one of the few people who will say this and mean this – but I liked dating! I've been in a serious relationship for many years now, however prior to this I did a lot of dating and liked the process very much. Here's why and here's what I did.

I held myself in high esteem and I was committed to presenting myself fearlessly as exactly who I am and how I look; in other words I chose to be authentic through the entire process. When you don't have anything to hide, nor are trying to make yourself appear to be someone you're not, everything is light and easy.

And I guess that's the other point –I really did enjoy a large percent of who I met. I found the men to be fascinating. I'm naturally social and a good listener and I enjoyed getting to know who they were and what made them tick. That was a good quality for dating. It allowed me to be present, be the real me and also be quite interested in who the other person was. I liked dating. I liked meeting them, getting to know them; the whole adventure.

The process was good. I feel that because I was honest it allowed me to have honest and good connections. It gave me a leg up on the process starting there. And it worked because I did meet the love of my life, who I am still with now, all of that interesting adventure led up to my relationship with HIM. I self-esteemed my way into my right relationship. My secret to great self-esteem is to like and be yourself. If you present the real you, you may not be for everyone (none of us are) but you will be for some people for sure. Just know you're interesting, funny, smart and cool to be with, then decide who you choose to spend time with. It's always a two-way street. Always know how worthwhile you are.

Deborah Dachinger
Award-Winning Radio Talk Show Host,
"Dare to Dream" Radio
www.deborahdachinger.com

ഈ ഈ ഈ

Dear Kelly,

My secret to great self-esteem is knowing that I am loved, and knowing that I am beautiful inside and out. I celebrate every success, tiny or large, and I have created a supportive environment for my mind, body and spirit. And finally, I choose to be happy and express my joy wherever I go.

Elizabeth Clark
Author and Trainer
www.yourtimetoshine.com
www.deliberateabundance.com

CHAPTER 17

WALK WITH YOUR HEAD HELD HIGH

"You can be You and I can be Me" ~ Kelly Falardeau

I know this can be a difficult thing to do, walking out the door no matter what. I learned that I had no choice. There have been times when people would tell me they overheard someone saying (about me), *"There's no way I would go out in public looking like her."* Or a few times they even said it to my husband.

Whenever I heard that, I just get blown away that people could be so rude to say something like that. Who are they to judge who can walk out the door looking like whatever they do? Who are they to think that everyone has to look a certain way in order to walk out the door and face the public?

I get extremely annoyed when people think there is a certain type of perception that people have to live up to in order to go out in public. Seriously, what other option did I have? Hide in the house forever?

My family was never ashamed of me. In fact, my grandma told me of an incident when a friend of hers said, *"You take her out in public?"* And my grandma said, *"Of course we do, she is our granddaughter, we love her, we are not ashamed of her."*

My mom was given a very strict order from my doctor that if she didn't treat me like a "normal" child, he would have me taken away from her. He made sure that she put me in school and took me places and didn't hide me from the public.

I believe that we don't have to live up to society's ideals of what we should look like in order to walk out the door. It shouldn't matter if we have scars or wear glasses or walk with a limp or are in a wheel chair, we deserve to go out in public.

I'll never forget when I was in junior high school and it wasn't accepted to wear dresses to school. If you did, you knew that you were going to be uncomfortable, teased or whispered about and/or get sly looks. And so, twice a year, I would do it anyways. I would break out of my comfort zone knowing that I was going to be whispered about even more so than I already was.

Those days were the toughest days of the year. I don't know why I would subject myself to that inner cruelty I felt, but I would. I still remember getting on the bus wondering who was going to give me the sly looks. Some of my biggest teasers were on my bus.

I remember walking down the halls feeling extreme discomfort and I would notice the looks I was getting. And usually by the end of the day, one girl would say to me, "*You look nice today.*" And I would say, "*Thank you, not sure why I'm wearing this dress and making myself feel like crap, but I am.*" I knew she understood because she felt the same way on her day. And then I would feel a little bit of comfort because not everyone in the whole school thought I was a dork for wearing a dress to school that day.

She was also one of the ones who would subject herself to the inner and outer cruelty by wearing a dress twice a year. She knew what I was feeling and wanted me to know it was okay. But I got through it knowing that school was just a short time of my life. I knew that when school ended, the boundaries would be lifted and I'd be able to wear whatever I wanted and without those cruel inner feelings that people made me feel with their stares and whispers just because I was wearing a dress. My family didn't give me an option of whether I wanted to go to school or not, they wouldn't allow me to hide at home just because I was burnt. That just wasn't a good enough excuse to not go out in public.

Yes, I was teased and stared at ALOT, but I learned to ignore it. I learned to stop judging what I thought people were thinking of me. I had to. There was no way I'd be able to feel great about me if I was to constantly think about what others thought of me and whether they thought I was ugly or not.

In fact, it actually bothers people who are with me more than me. I am so used to ignoring people's stares that I don't notice it much anymore.

My best friend was telling me about how upset he was when we were walking down the street in Banff together. He was noticing people staring at me and I didn't notice anyone staring at me. I asked him what was wrong and he said, *"I'm trying not to notice all the people staring at you, I just want to slap them, they're making me so mad. How can they be so cruel to you, isn't it bothering you?"* And I said *"Nope, I'm not even noticing it, don't worry so much about me it doesn't bother me and I'll never see them again anyways."*

So now I want to tell you a funny story about me. This story will explain how I'm able to walk out the door no matter what. Whenever I speak about inner beauty, I usually tell my "pigtail story" and people just laugh when I tell it.

I just love when women wear pigtails. I think they look so cute, but I never had the guts to do it. I thought people would think I was crazy if I wore pigtails and so I couldn't do it.

We used to take our kids swimming quite often and every time I came out of the pool, I look like a drowned rat and I hated it. My hair was everywhere, my bald spot was showing and I always seemed to forget my hair brush and blow dryer and then when my hair dried, I looked like a cave woman. Yeah, not a pretty picture at all and I hated it.

And it never failed that we needed to stop at the grocery store and pick up something for supper after swimming. I'll never forget one time when Max said, *"Ok, run in real quick and grab a few things, I'll wait in the van with the kids so we don't have to park."* And I said, *"Seriously, you want me to run into the store looking like a drowned rat? You're bald, you go."*

One time when we were going to the water park for the twins' birthday party, I decided I was going to be brave and put in pigtails like all the other cute pigtail girls. So I put in the pigtails and looked in the mirror and said to myself, *"Wow, do you ever look CUTE in those pigtails."* Yes, I did say that, I really thought I looked cute.

So then Max came upstairs and said, *"You know your bald spot is showing."* And I said *"Yeah, so what?"* And he said, *"Well, I really wish you wouldn't wear the pigtails or find a way to cover it so your bald spot doesn't show."* And I said, *"So what if anyone sees my bald spot, I don't care, I think I look cute and I'm wearing the pigtails, you're bald and you go out the door, why shouldn't I be able to go out the door with cute pigtails even with my bald spot showing? Do you think someone is going to have the guts to come up to me and say hey lady your bald spot is showing? And if they don't like my bald spot showing, they can just turn around. Nope, and so what if they do, I look cute and I feel great, I'm going to the water park this way."*

I went to the water park that day and for once I didn't feel like a drowned rat. I felt great and it didn't matter to me what other people thought. I couldn't see people staring at my bald spot – it's in the back of my head. How would I notice them staring?

You see, here's what I was thinking:

I feel cute, why shouldn't I go out the door this way? So what if people are going to stare. Why should I take the pigtails out just because it's going to make someone else feel more comfortable, I feel greater than great? If I take the pigtails out, I'm going to feel insecure and crappy and feel like a drowned rat AGAIN.

Another staring story was when I was only 23-years-old; I was still a size zero and didn't have any kids yet. Max and I were going to a wedding that day and there was time in-between the wedding and dinner, so we were walking down the street killing time.

Max was wearing a suit looking pretty handsome and I was wearing a cute dress. Max was holding my hand and two guys were walking towards us. They were staring at me and as they walked by the one guy said, *"Wow, isn't he a lucky guy, look at the hot girl he's with, you can tell he's in love."*

Another story was when I decided I could finally walk out the door wearing a hat. My friend put a hat on me and said, *"Wow, don't you look cute."* And I said, *"Yeah, it does look cute on me."* So I went and bought a hat similar to the one she had.

One morning, I was going to volunteer at a friend's trade show and so I put on my favorite jeans, a funky shirt and heels. Then I put my hair in pigtails and put on my new hat. I looked in the mirror and said, *"Wow, now don't you look cute today."* And walked out the door.

When I got there, I was shocked! I couldn't believe all the comments I got. A bunch of my friends said, *"Wow, Kel, you look great today, love the hat!"* Even people I didn't know stopped and told me how cute I looked. And every compliment I got made me feel greater than great.

So then I started talking to another friend of mine and she said, *"Wow, Kel, you look fantastic today, and not just the hat, but the heels, the jeans, the funky top, the whole package.*" Then she told me that she had put a hat on that morning too, but couldn't walk out the door with it on. She didn't have the confidence to walk out the door. I was surprised.

ACTION STEPS:

Find the courage to wear something you normally wouldn't be able to wear (but love) and see what people say. You never know, you may get compliments.

SECRET:

If you feel greater than great, then walk out the door no matter what others think.

Dear Kelly:

One of my favorite quotes is by Oscar Wilde, who says "Be yourself, everyone else is already taken."

This is such a powerful statement and certainly has a great deal to do with self-esteem. As a former correctional officer and mediator, I frequently saw people trying to be someone else, instead of bringing their true self to the world. Now as an international speaker, I help individuals and workplaces be more inspired and resilient.

When you try to be someone or something you are not, it is incongruent. You will feel it and so will those around you. Showing up this way results in people comparing themselves to one another, or expending energy to be someone else instead of being the best version of you. When you bring the best version of YOU to the world, the world will be a better place. Life will be easier, there will be less resistance, and the world will experience you! Thank you Kelly for bringing your best version of YOU to the world, you are making a difference!

Charmaine Hammond, MA, BA
www.hammondgroup.biz
www.ontobysterms.com

Dear Kelly,

Being a burn survivor since the age of six when a water heater explosion caused burns to 85% of my body; growing up was quite difficult with all the teasing. My parents taught me a very important message and I carry it with me to this day.... "Believe in yourself and others will also believe in you. Hold your head high and be proud of who you are."

These positive messages are how I have lived my life. I believe self-esteem or positive self-image comes from within. First and foremost you have to learn to love your body for everything it is in spite of a physical difference. Until you learn to love yourself unconditionally no one else will ever be able to love you. I have always believed that if I project a positive self-image others will see that in me. It is so important that you begin to identify how you view yourself independent of the often negative interactions you may have with others in society.

Believe me, this does take some work and does not happen overnight. Be patient with yourself but start taking steps to accomplish your goals. Try not to use your past accomplishments as a way to determine what is acceptable today. Set small goals. Take baby steps. It doesn't have to be big, but it has to be there to celebrate successes. Stop all the negative self-talk about yourself and replace it with high-energy positive talk.

So I will leave you with this.... Are you confident in your body? Are you comfortable in your skin? Are there physical differences that bother you and what are you going to do about it??

As Eleanor Roosevelt said, "No one can make you feel inferior without your permission."

Cindy Rutter

Judgment

I am not always proud of where my feet
have taken me
I have walked in places most people
could not understand
I have been through my own hell and back
maybe you have too
my feet have carried me through places
of great joy as well
please do not look at me strange
or judge me because my feet have carried me to places
you have not been or understand
I mean no harm to you and your loved ones
I only ask that you love me today
not for where my feet have taken me
but for where they are going.

By Daniel Gutierrez

Dear Kelly,

Many times in life I have felt that there were eyes staring right through my soul. I felt judged by everyone, even the dog. When I wrote this poem I didn't have the wisdom that I have today. I was hurt and devastated that a friend could judge me the way they had without even knowing where my life had taken me and that I wanted them to see where I was headed, not where I had been. I am sure you have felt that way too.

The reality is that today I know that no one person, place or thing defines me, but has the capacity for me to look deeper within for the answers to life, I seek. I have the capacity to decide what my self-esteem is going to be!

Self-esteem is defined as overall evaluation or appraisal of his or her own worth. Perfect! That means that I define what that is. Most of my life I let others define that and with my thoughts I made it all true. Right here, right now! Today I don't allow any thoughts that are not true stay in my thoughts, not even for a second! We are all born to manifest the greatness in us... not only in some of us but all of us. We are born in the image of Greatness and therefore like the rays of the sun that cannot be separated from the sun, we cannot be separated from God/Source/Universe.

I completely understand that today that my most dominate thought is manifested into the reality that I see today. What is your most dominate thought about you? That is how you are manifesting your self-esteem. You want power, be powerful, you want love, BE loveable, you want wealth, BE and feel abundant. Get it?

So the secret? There is no secret. It's not out there somewhere, its going inward and making the most important trip you will ever make...from the head to the heart. That my friend is where you will find all the answers to your life and affairs. That is where every need is met, every problem is solved, every question is answered. The answer to self-esteem is YOU. Namaste!

Daniel Gutierrez
Author, Speaker, World Transformational Leader and Radio Personality
www.danielgutierrez.com
www.primernetwork.org

ॐ ॐ ॐ

Dear Kelly,

My secret to self-esteem is simply not taking myself too seriously. I can laugh off just about anything that goes awry because it really won't matter later (i.e., in a minute, an hour, a day or a year . . . who remembers or cares?). And I know I can live through just about anything tough and scary, because I already have. "Been there, done that" is actually a very liberating place to hang out.

*But here's my real secret; you've heard about being between a rock and a hard place? I'll take the ROCK any day. ROCK is **R**esilience, **O**ptimism, **C**ourage and **K**indness. These are the watchwords that run my life, hold me up, and make me who I am. They are also the foundation of the legacy I will leave (we all leave one, it might as well ROCK!).*

With love and admiration,

Deborah Brown
Author, Speaker and Co-Host of
The Boomer and the Babe Show
www.BoomerandTheBabe.com

Bonus Chapter
You Have a Grand Destiny!
And, it's Happening Right Now!
Marsh Engle

To live our most amazing life is about discovering ways to bring our greatest passion and purpose to life! And, I've found that the best way to accomplish this is to create a solid practice to nurture my creative connection. Here's a list of 20 methods I use to optimize confidence, ignite flow, and stretch for my highest potential every day!

1. Take a 10-30-minute walk every day. And while you walk, smile – it's the direct path to feeling more connected with yourself, with others and with your surroundings.

2. Sit in silence for at least 10-minutes each day. The benefits are priceless!

3. Start your day with success in mind. When you wake up in the morning, make it part of your routine to speak aloud your intention – the feeling tone that you wish to create for the day.

4. Make it a point to bring more joy in your life each day. Read poetry, call a friend, listen to music, take a walk in nature, explore a new subject. Whatever brings you joy, commit to living more of it!

5. Dedicate time to strengthening your spiritual practice: Meditation, yoga, tai chi, chanting, prayer. This is the ultimate fuel for a rich, prosperous life.

6. Invest time with people who are motivated, inspiring, encouraging, insightful and fun.

7. Create a practice of exploring. Ask lots of questions. And, listen for the answers.

8. Place nutrition high on your list. Eat more living foods. Drink plenty of water.

9. De-clutter your home, your car and your desk. Let go of the old. Let in the new!

10. Value the power of your spoken word. Don't waste your precious energy on gossip, long conversations about the past or things you cannot control. Rather invest your words in empowered thoughts, solutions and focused outcomes.

11. Look for the yes in all things. Focus on the ways that every experience is expanding your connection with yourself, with others and with life.

12. Surround yourself with people who challenge you to be your very best. Allow yourself to receive the wisdom of mentors and the lessons of role models.

13. Value your greatest talents and share them relentlessly with others.

14. Make peace with your past and empower your present.

15. Remember comparison compromises self-worth. Don't fall into the habit of comparing yourself or your life to others. Celebrate your unique and grand design.

16. Create a sacred space for yourself. Light candles, treat yourself to nice linens, listen to music. Make it a point to be surrounded by beauty.

17. Practice the mantra: "No one is in charge of my happiness except me."

18. Waste not one moment! Forgive yourself and forgive everyone for everything.

19. Life is ALWAYS changing! However the situation, one thing is certain: It will change!

20. You have a grand destiny unfolding. And, it's happening right now!

Marsh Engle

Author, facilitator, coach and founder of Amazing Woman's Day www.MarshEngle.com

Self-esteem, or lack thereof, is learned. If it can be learned, then it can be taught.

Webster's Dictionary defines self-esteem as "belief in oneself." If you choose to believe the truths about your value as a human being not what you do or your current skills, education or financial situation, you will have belief in yourself. As that belief increases, you will find that your ability to accomplish anything you desire increases.

Another word for self-esteem is pride. The definition of pride is, "proper respect for oneself, a sense of one's own worth." My main mentor taught this, "If you know the truth, it will set you free." It is crucial that you discover the truth about your value as a person, a friend, a brother or sister, wife or husband, father or mother.

Make a list of all the things about you that you don't like...things that are not okay or are failings. Then get together with two or three friends, include your spouse if you are married and ask them to help you create a list of everything good they can see in you. You are reliable; you are kind, your fun etc. Even the little things like you say excuse me after burping etc.

Their list will be far longer than yours. Decide to believe their list. Does that mean your list is to be ignored? Of course not, but it does mean you should start seeing yourself properly, truthfully. If you have a nice car with a dent or two in it, you don't focus only on the dents. Same with yourself.

Give this brief quiz your honest answers:

- Does it matter how others perceive you?
- Will their perspective of you have an effect on your life?
- Will how they see you affect your income positively or negatively?

- Will how you are viewed by others affect your social life?
- Will it affect your ability to attract a mate?
- Will it affect your marriage?
- Will it affect your children?
- Will it affect your confidence?
- Does how people perceive you affect your happiness?

If you answered "yes" to all of these, you'd be right. How you perceive yourself is critical to your success and achievement in life....or your lack of it. How you act, talk, walk, dress and present yourself has an effect on all aspects of your life, as does how others perceive you. Self-image can have a major influence on such things as finding a spouse, earning an impressive income or getting involved with life in general and getting the maximum out of it.

When I ask people what they think it means to acquire a good self-image in the physical area of their lives, I usually hear "get in shape...lose weight...lift weights...get some kind of cosmetic surgery." Occasionally, I hear that they want to learn self-defense. Some say they want new clothes etc.

Sociologists did an experiment to see which mattered the most, impressions or skill. They sent 15 actors and 15 highly skilled professionals to apply for the same jobs including accounting positions. The actors usually knew little or nothing about the job duties but he or she faked the knowledge. More often than not the actor – not the qualified person – got the job offer. That happened because actors are excellent at making good impressions. They know all about posture, body language, dressing for success, inflection in language and facial expression etc. This underscores the need for everyone to learn to do the same for optimal success in life.

I remember being fairly new in the business world. I was really struggling financially. Luckily I had learned about the significance and power of a proper appearance. A potential client made a very strong statement to me that I have never forgotten. As she sat in my office, she said, "Jack, you're obviously successful and that gives me a lot of comfort in doing business with you." I asked her why she felt that way.

She answered this way: "Well, Jack, you look successful. You have a great office, you sound successful, you sound confident, and so I assume that you are." That experience is a main reason I always wear a nice suit when meeting with a potential client.

An Important Tip: If your personal appearance is a turn-off, it will never matter to most people if you've got a ton of talent and ability. Your appearance and personality is the way you package yourself. People rarely stop and bother to find out exactly what the contents inside an unattractive package are like. It's a turn-off.

Of course, ability and performance are what really determines whether you keep a client (or job) or not, but a great deal of ability can be completely obscured behind your personal appearance. Keep in mind that ability may never be recognized or tested if a person's poor or negative personal appearance is a turn-off or indication of mediocrity or non-professional attitude.

While undoubtedly there are exceptions to this rule, take it as true, that there are thousands of people who are continually limited—a self-imposed limit in many instances—because they don't present a sharp personal appearance.

The phrase, "You never get a second chance to make a first impression," is true and many times it's fatal to the desired end results that you're seeking. Appropriate outward appearance dramatically affects both you and those you come in contact with.

Esteem for oneself is very important to acquire. Decide today that you are going to see yourself properly and show the world that you are a great person inside and out....with some flaws.

Jack M. Zufelt
"Mentor to Millions"
Author of the #1 best selling book'
The DNA of Success
www.dnaofsuccess.com
(FREE video there for you)

Here's What I Know:

Just like with my last book, 'No Risk No Rewards'; I ended the book with random thoughts about what I've learned over the course of my life. Here are my random thoughts about self-esteem.

My great self-esteem:

- didn't come from **any** bottle, not a make-up bottle, a magic bottle, a shampoo bottle or even a bottle filled with alcohol

- didn't come from when I used to call myself the ugly scar-faced girl

- didn't come from when I used to watch all the negative news on television

- or when I used to watch horror movies and fill up my head with junk

- it didn't come from when I concentrated on everybody staring at me and thinking I was ugly

- it didn't come from when I used to gossip about people

- it didn't happen when I listened to negative people and not positive ones

- nor did it come when I kept finding the negatives in people and picking out what was wrong about them

- it didn't come from when I used to constantly pick on myself and tell myself that I wasn't good enough, I wasn't successful enough, I wasn't pretty enough

- it didn't come from me worrying about what everyone else thought of me

- it didn't come when I couldn't accept me for who I was

- it didn't come from when I used to work at a job that I was miserable at

- nor did it come when I saw only obstacles and not possibilities

- it didn't come from being jealous of other people's success

- it didn't come from me hiding my dreams and thinking I didn't deserve them

- it also didn't develop overnight – it took me years to feel greater than great

- it didn't come from when people tried to stop me from following my dreams

- it didn't come when I wasn't grateful for what I already had

- it didn't come from when I was beating myself up because I wasn't as successful as my friends and family were

- I didn't get it when I was chasing business opportunities that weren't my passion

- it didn't come when I gave up on me

- it didn't come when I didn't trust myself

- it didn't come when I was trying to please 'others' before 'me'

- it didn't come from wearing make-up that didn't make me feel beautiful

- I didn't get it when I was trying to be perfect

- I didn't get it when I was trying to be someone other than me

- It didn't come when I blamed others for my failures

- It didn't come when I was constantly complaining about my life

- It didn't come when I didn't have an "attitude of gratitude"

My self-esteem came from everything I did in this book and from my heart and soul; and when I discovered my two ultimate secrets:

*Self-esteem doesn't come in **any** kind of bottle*

and

*You need to learn how to make yourself feel **greater than great**, not like crap.*

Celebrating the baby boomer woman

The
Fabulous@50
Martini

Every good martini should have flavour, sparkle and something to make
your lips pucker. Ingredients: Plenty of fabulous women 40-60.Vibrant
website with blogs, a marketplace and a free newsletter.
Diamond membership with gifts and benefits. Be Fabulous!
Magazine, with stories on fashion, food, travel, sex,
finances for the baby boomer women.
Fabulous@50 Experience & Martini
Party - a tradeshow with a twist.
Put all the ingredients into
a mixing glass filled
with happiness,
stir for 30
seconds.
S t r a i n
into an
a b u n -
d a n t l y
chilled
martini
g l a s s ,
add a
d a s h
of fun,
a n d
g a r -
n i s h
w i t h
inspi-
r a -
tion,
g r a t i -
tude, and a splash
of love and kindness.

www.fabulousat50.com

Today's.
Businesswoman
magazine

To Educate, Encourage and Equip Women
in Kingdom Businesses

God is Calling You...

How will YOU respond?

Subscribe today

$**48**CDN one-year subscription/
4 issues
(includes shipping/handling)

www.
TodaysBusinesswomanMagazine
.com

email:
TodaysBusinesswoman@shaw.ca

www.TodaysBusinessWomanMagazine.com

email: TodaysBusinessWoman@shaw.ca

144

Online Exposure and Publicity Don't Come in a Bottle...

But They Are Easier To Get Than You May Think!
Create a vibrant, positive, and healthy business persona that magnetizes people by commanding a strong media presence.

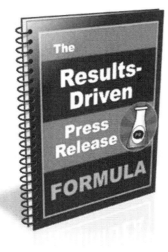

Claim your *free* copy of "The Results-Driven Press Release Formula" and learn the secrets of gaining online publicity and visibility in the digital age:
http://www.onlineprnews.com/how-to-write-a-press-release

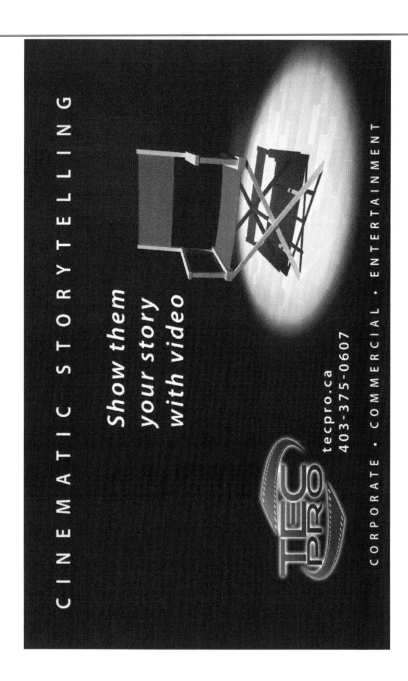

146

COPE 2 HOPE

Learn how to Heal
Within, by
From Meditation &
using Visualization...

" Have you suffered from Sexual or
Emotional, Physical to heal
Abuse? Do you want a new
the past, and rewrite it today?
future for yourself today?

" Contact Carrie Kohan
for Cope 2 Hope 2nd/or Group
Consultations Workshops/
Wellness Workshops!

" 780-298-0788

carrie.kohan@gmail.com
http://www.cope2hope.com

" Motivational Speaker / Facilitator/
2001 UN & Gov't of
Counselor / 2001 Contribution
Canada Award for Distinction
2010 YWCA Women of Advocacy
Recipient for Advocacy

Body by Vi™
CHALLENGE

LOSE WEIGHT ✦ GET HEALTHY ✦ WIN PRIZES ✦ EARN MONEY

WHAT IS **YOUR** 90 DAY GOAL?

www.scooby.bodybyvi.com

VINCE SKUBLENY

Cell: 780.289.9855   Email: vscooby@gmail.com

Independent Distributor

VISALUS®

LIFE ✦ HEALTH ✦ PROSPERITY

About Kelly

Kelly Falardeau is an author, entrepreneur and a motivational speaker. Friends, family and those who have worked with Kelly all say that she doesn't let fear stop her – when she wants to achieve something, she just does it. They also say that the fact that Kelly is a burn survivor since she was two-years-old is so motivating because she does not let circumstances dictate her success.

At 21, she was nominated and won the position of President of the Alberta Burn Rehabilitation Society. As a kid, she also won the 4-H Most Improved Member award plus various public speaking awards and even the fastest senior typist award in high school.

Kelly has been featured on TV in Canada such as Global TV Edmonton and Calgary, CTS TV, CTV TV, Breakfast TV, Access TV, CBC, A-Channel and CFRN. She has also appeared as a guest on various radio shows too. Articles have been written about her in the Edmonton Woman Magazine, Edmonton Examiner, Edmonton Journal, Edmonton Sun, Pioneer Balloons Balloon Magazine and she also won the MOM Executive Officer award plus the Fierce Woman of the Year award from the MOM Magazine.

Kelly was chosen amongst thousands to present her business to the Dragons for the Dragons' Den television. Kelly was selected out of 1500-women to compete in the Every Woman model search competition. She faced her fear of being judged by her appearance and walked the plank and won the Peoples' Choice award.

She is a sought–after international speaker because of her ability to engage others. She is able to move audience's emotions and make them see how a bad situation can become a great one. She will have you crying, laughing and dancing in your chairs as she shares her many stories about risks/rewards, inner beauty and self-esteem. Her "beauty exercise" is a dynamite experience that shows teenagers and adults where their true beauty comes from. She is also the author of 'No Risk No Rewards.'

To book Kelly for your next event, email her at mykellyf@gmail.com or visit her website at: www.mykellyf.com or blog: http://blog.mykellyf.com